The Freedom Philosophy

The Freedom Philosophy

The Foundation for Economic Education, Inc.
Irvington-on-Hudson, New York 10533

About the Publisher

The Foundation for Economic Education, founded in 1946 by Leonard E. Read, exists to serve individuals concerned about freedom. Recognizing that the real reasons for freedom are grasped only through an understanding of the free market, private property, limited government way of life, The Foundation is a first-source institution providing literature and activities presenting this point of view.

The Freeman, a monthly study journal of ideas on liberty, has been published by The Foundation since 1956. Its articles and essays offer timeless ideas on the positive case for human liberty and criticisms of the failures of collectivism. *The Freeman* is available to anyone upon request.

Published March 1988

ISBN-0-910614-75-x

Copyright © by

The Foundation for Economic Education, Inc.

Permission granted to reprint without special request except "Free Enterprise: The Key to Prosperity," "The Source of Rights," and "Isaiah's Job."

Printed in U.S.A.

2nd Printing   January 1990

The Freedom Philosophy

I. Freedom: An Overview

II. In the Market Place

III. Political Aspects

IV. Moral Foundation

V. Personal Practice

VI. In Retrospect and Prospect

Part One

Freedom: An Overview

The purpose of The Foundation for Economic Education (FEE) is to explore and explain the freedom philosophy. That's why Leonard Read started FEE in 1946 and why the effort persists with growing vigor as the decades pass.

The freedom philosophy has been outlined as "the free market, private property, limited government way of life." But more than that bare outline is needed for the enlightened personal practice of freedom. So here is an attempt to bring together in handy, readable form some of the best thoughts of serious students of liberty. Many others, of course, over the centuries, have contributed to the ever-growing library on the topic. The essays here are selected as an introduction and guide for anyone who would pursue the study.

The opening essay is slightly condensed from a lecture Leonard Read adapted and delivered to hundreds of audiences dating back to 1961. It affords an overview of the philosophy which will be examined in more detail in later chapters.

1

The Essence of Americanism

by Leonard E. Read

Delivered as a speech in 1961.

Someone once said: It isn't that Christianity has been tried and found wanting; it has been tried and found difficult—and abandoned. Perhaps the same thing might be said about freedom. The American people are becoming more and more afraid of, and are running away from, their own revolution. I think that statement takes a bit of documentation.

I would like to go back, a little over three centuries in our history, to the year 1620, which was the occasion of the landing of our Pilgrim Fathers at Plymouth Rock. That little colony began its career in a condition of pure and unadulterated communism. For it made no difference how much or how little any member of that colony produced; all the produce went into a common warehouse under authority, and the proceeds of the warehouse were doled out in accordance with the authority's idea of need. In short, the Pilgrims began the practice of a principle held up by Karl Marx two centuries later as the ideal of the Communist Party: From each according to ability, to each according to need—and by force!

There was a good reason why these communalistic or communistic practices were discontinued. It was because the members of the Pilgrim colony were starving and dying. As a rule, that type of experience causes people to stop and think about it!

Anyway, they did stop and think about it. During the third winter Governor Bradford got together with the remaining members of the colony and said to them, in effect: "This coming spring we are going to try a new idea. We are going to drop the practice of 'from each according to ability, to each according to need.' We are going to try the idea of 'to each according to merit.'" And when Governor Bradford said that, he enunciated the private property principle as clearly and succinctly as any economist ever had. That principle is nothing more nor less than each individual having a right to the fruits of his own labor. Next spring came, and it was observed that not only was father in the field but mother and the children were there, also. Governor Bradford records that "Any generall wante or famine hath not been amongst them since to this day."

It was by reason of the practice of this private property principle that there began in this country an era of growth and development which sooner or later had to lead to revolutionary political ideas. And it did lead to what I refer to as the real American revolution.

I do not think of the real American revolution as the armed conflict we had with King George III. That was a reasonably minor fracas as such fracases go! The real American revolution was a novel concept or idea which broke with the whole political history of the world.

Up until 1776 men had been contesting with each other, killing each other by the millions, over the age-old question of which of the numerous forms of authoritarianism—that is, man-made authority—should preside as sovereign over man. And then, in 1776, in the fraction of one sentence written into the Declaration of Independence was stated the real American Revolution, the new idea, and it was this: "that all men are created equal; that they are endowed by their Creator with certain unalienable Rights; that among these are Life, Liberty and the pursuit of Happiness." That was it. This is the essence of Americanism. This is the rock upon which the whole "American miracle" was founded.

This revolutionary concept was at once a spiritual, a political, and an economic concept. It was spiritual in that the writers of the Declaration recognized and publicly proclaimed that the Creator was the endower of man's rights, and thus the Creator is sovereign.

It was political in implicitly denying that the state is the endower of man's rights, thus declaring that the state is not sovereign.

It was economic in the sense that if an individual has a right to his life, it follows that he has a right to sustain his life—the sustenance of life being nothing more nor less than the fruits of one's own labor.

It is one thing to state such a revolutionary concept as this; it's quite another thing to implement it—to put it into practice. To accomplish this, our Founding Fathers added two political instruments—the Constitution and the Bill of Rights. These two instruments were essentially a set of prohibitions; prohibitions not against the people but against the thing the people, from their Old World experience, had learned to fear, namely, over-extended government.

Benefits of Limited Government

The Constitution and the Bill of Rights more severely limited government than government had ever before been limited in the history of the world. And there were benefits that flowed from this severe limitation of the state.

Number one, there wasn't a single person who turned to the government for security, welfare, or prosperity because government was so limited that it had nothing on hand to dispense, nor did it then have the power to take from some that it might give to others. To what or to whom do people turn if they cannot turn to government for security, welfare, or prosperity? They turn where they should turn—to themselves.

As a result of this discipline founded on the concept that the Creator, not the state, is the endower of man's rights, we developed in this country on an unprecedented scale a quality of character that Emerson referred to as "self-reliance." All over the world the American people gained the reputation of being self-reliant.

There was another benefit that flowed from this severe limitation of government. When government is limited to the inhibition of the destructive actions of men—that is, when it is limited to inhibiting fraud and depredation, violence and misrepresentation, when it is limited to invoking a common justice—then there is no organized force standing against the productive or creative actions of citizens. As a consequence of this limitation on government, there occurred a freeing, a releasing, of creative human energy, on an unprecedented scale.

This was the combination mainly responsible for the "American miracle," founded on the belief that the Creator, not the state, is the endower of man's rights.

This manifested itself among the people as individual freedom of choice. People had freedom of choice as to how they employed themselves. They had freedom of choice as to what they did with the fruits of their own labor.

But something happened to this remarkable idea of ours, this revolutionary concept. It seems that the people we placed in government office as our agents made a discovery. Having acquisitive instincts for affluence and power over others—as indeed some of us do—they discovered that the force which inheres in government, which the people had delegated to them in order to inhibit the destructive actions of man, this monopoly of force could be used to invade the productive and creative areas in society—one of which is the business sector. And they also found that if they incurred any deficits by their interventions, the same government force could be used to collect the wherewithal to pay the bills.

I would like to suggest to you that the extent to which government in America has departed from the original design of inhibiting the destructive actions of man and invoking a common justice; the extent to which government has invaded the productive and creative areas; the extent to which the government in this country has assumed the responsibility for the security, welfare, and prosperity of our people is a measure of the extent to which socialism and communism have developed here in this land of ours.

The Lengthening Shadow

Can we measure this development? Not precisely, but we can get a fair idea of it by referring to something I said a moment ago about one of our early characteristics as a nation—individual freedom of choice as to the use of the fruits of one's own labor. If you will measure the loss in freedom of choice in this matter, you will get an idea of what is going on.

There was a time, about 120 years ago, when the average citizen had somewhere between 95 and 98 per cent freedom of choice with each of his income dollars. That was because the tax take of the government—federal, state, and local—was between 2 and 5 per cent of the earned income of the people. But, as the emphasis shifted from this earlier design, as government began to move in to invade the productive and creative areas and to assume the responsibility for the security, welfare, and prosperity of the people, the percentage of the take of the people's earned income increased. The percentage of the take kept going up and up and up until today it's not 2 to 5 per cent. It is now [1961] over 35 per cent.

Whenever the take of the people's earned income by government reaches a certain level—20 or 25 per cent—it is no longer politically expedient to pay for the costs of government by direct tax levies. Governments then resort to inflation as a means of financing their ventures. This is happening to us now! By "inflation" I mean increasing the volume of money by the national government's fiscal policy. Governments resort to inflation with popular support because the people apparently are naive enough to believe that they can have their cake and eat it, too. Many people do not realize that they cannot continue to enjoy so-called "benefits" from government without having to pay for them. They do not appreciate the fact that inflation is probably the most unjust and most cruel tax of all.

Inflation is the fiscal concomitant of socialism or the welfare state or state interventionism—call it what you will. Inflation is a political weapon. There are no other means of financing the welfare state except by inflation.

So, if you don't like inflation, there is only one thing you can do: assist in returning our government to its original principles.

One of my hobbies is cooking and, therefore, I am familiar with the gadgets around the kitchen. One of the things with which I am familiar is a sponge. A sponge in some respects resembles a good economy. A sponge will sop up an awful lot of mess; but when the sponge is saturated, the sponge itself is a mess, and the only way you can make it useful again is to wring the mess out of it. I hope my analogy is clear.

Inflation in the United States has ever so many more catastrophic potentials than has ever been the case in any other country in history. We here are the most advanced division-of-labor society that has ever existed. That is, we are more specialized than any other people has ever been; we are further removed from self-subsistence.

Indeed, we are so specialized today that every one of us— everybody in this room, in the nation, even the farmer—is absolutely dependent upon a free, uninhibited exchange of our numerous specialties. That is a self-evident fact.

Destroying the Circulatory System

In any highly specialized economy you do not effect specialized exchanges by barter. You never observe a man going into a gasoline station saying, "Here is a goose; give me a gallon of gas." That's not the way to do it in a specialized economy. You use an economic circulatory system, which is money, the medium of exchange.

This economic circulatory system, in some respects, can be likened to the circulatory system of the body, which is the blood stream.

The circulatory system of the body picks up oxygen in the lungs and ingested food in the mid-section and distributes these specialties to the 30 trillion cells of the body. At those points it picks up carbon dioxide and waste matter and carries them off. I could put a hypodermic needle into one of your veins and thin your blood stream to the point where it would no longer make these exchanges, and when I reached that point, we could refer to you quite accurately in the past tense.

By the same token, you can thin your economic circulatory system, your medium of exchange, to the point where it will no longer circulate the products and services of economic specialization.

Those of you who are interested in doing something about this, have a right to ask yourselves a perfectly logical question: Has there ever been an instance, historically, when a country has been on this toboggan and succeeded in reversing itself? There have been some minor instances. I will not attempt to enumerate them. The only significant one took place in England after the Napoleonic Wars.

How England Did It

England's debt, in relation to her resources, was larger than ours is now; her taxation was confiscatory; restrictions on the exchanges of goods and services were numerous, and there were strong controls on production and prices. Had it not been for the smugglers, many people would have starved!

Something happened in that situation, and we ought to take cognizance of it. What happened there might be emulated here even though our problem is on a much larger scale. There were in England such men as John Bright and Richard Cobden, men who understood the principle of freedom of exchange. Over in France, there was a politician by the name of Chevalier, and an economist named Frederic Bastiat.

Incidentally, if any of you have not read the little book by Bastiat entitled *The Law,* I commend it as the finest thing that I have ever read on the principles one ought to keep in mind when trying to judge for oneself what the scope of government should be.

Bastiat was feeding his brilliant ideas to Cobden and Bright, and these men were preaching the merits of freedom of exchange. Members of Parliament listened and, as a consequence, there began the greatest reform movement in British history.

Parliament repealed the Corn Laws, which here would be like repealing subsidies to farmers. They repealed the Poor Laws, which here would be like repealing Social Security. And fortunately for them they had a monarch—her name was Victoria—who relaxed the authority that the English people themselves believed to be implicit in her office. She gave them freedom in the sense that a prisoner on parole has freedom, a permissive kind of freedom but with lots of latitude. Englishmen, as a result, roamed all over the world achieving unparalleled prosperity and building an enlightened empire.

This development continued until just before World War I. Then the same old political disease set in again. What precisely is this disease that causes inflation and all these other troubles? It has many popular names, some of which I have mentioned, such as socialism, communism, state interventionism, and welfare statism. It has other names such as fascism and Nazism. It has some local names like New Deal, Fair Deal, New Republicanism, New Frontier, and the like.

A Dwindling Faith in Freedom

If you will take a careful look at these so-called "progressive ideologies," you will discover that each of them has a characteristic common to all the rest. This common characteristic is a cell in the body politic which has a cancer-like capacity for inordinate growth. This characteristic takes the form of a belief. It is a rapidly growing belief in the use of organized force—government—not to carry out its original function of inhibiting the destructive actions of men and invoking a common justice, but to control the productive and creative activity of citizens in society. That is all it is. Check any one of these ideologies and see if this is not its essential characteristic.

Here is an example of what I mean: I can remember the time when, if we wanted a house or housing, we relied on private enterprise. First, we relied on the person who wanted a house. Second, we relied on the persons who wanted to compete in the building. And third, we relied on those who thought they saw some advantage to themselves in loaning the money for the tools, material, and labor. Under that system of free enterprise, Americans built more square feet of housing per person than any other country on the face of the earth. Despite that remarkable accomplishment, more and more people are coming to believe that the only way we can have adequate housing is to use government to take the earnings from some and give these earnings, in the form of housing, to others. In other words, we are right back where the Pilgrim Fathers were in 1620–23 and Karl Marx was in 1847—from each according to ability, to each according to need, and by the use of force.

As this belief in the use of force as a means of creative accomplishment increases, the belief in free men—that is, men acting freely, competitively, cooperatively, voluntarily—correspondingly diminishes. Increase compulsion and freedom declines. Therefore, the solution to this problem, if there be one, must take a positive form, namely, the restoration of a faith in what free men can accomplish. The American people, by and large, have lost track of the spiritual antecedent of the American miracle. You are given a choice: either you accept the idea of the Creator as the endower of man's rights, or you submit to the idea that the state is the endower of man's rights. I double-dare any of you to offer a third alternative. We have forgotten the real source of our rights and are suffering the consequences.

Millions of people, aware that something is wrong, look around for someone to blame. They dislike socialism and communism and give lip service to their dislike. They sputter about the New Frontier and Modern Republicanism. But, among the millions who say they don't like these ideologies, you cannot find one in ten thousand whom you yourself will designate as a skilled, accomplished expositor of socialism's opposite—the free market, private property, limited government philosophy with its moral and spiritual antecedents. How many people do you know who are knowledgeable in this matter? Very few, I dare say.

Developing Leadership

No wonder we are losing the battle! The problem then—the real problem—is developing a leadership for this philosophy, persons from different walks of life who understand and can explain this philosophy.

This leadership functions at three levels. The first level requires that an individual achieve that degree of understanding which makes it utterly impossible for him to have any hand in supporting or giving any encouragement to any socialistic activities. Leadership at this level doesn't demand any creative writing, thinking, and talking, but it does require an understanding of what things are really socialistic, however disguised. People reject socialism in name, but once any socialistic activity has been Americanized, nearly everybody thinks it's all right. So you have to take the definition of socialism—state ownership and control of the means of production—and check our current practices against this definition.

As a matter of fact, you should read the ten points of the *Communist Manifesto* and see how close we have come to achieving them right here in America. It's amazing.

The second level of leadership is reached when you achieve that degree of understanding and exposition which makes it possible to expose the fallacies of socialism and set forth some of the principles of freedom to those who come within your own personal orbit. Now, this takes a lot more doing.

One of the things you have to do to achieve this second level of leadership is some studying. Most people have to, at any rate, and one of the reasons the Foundation for Economic Education exists is to help such people. At the Foundation we are trying to understand the freedom philosophy better ourselves, and we seek ways of explaining it with greater clarity. The results appear in single page releases, in a monthly journal, in books and pamphlets, in lectures, seminars, and the like. Our journal, *The Freeman,* for instance, is available to anyone on request. We impose no other condition.

The third level of leadership is to achieve that excellence in understanding and exposition which will cause other persons to seek you out as a tutor. That is the highest you can go, but there is no limit as to how far you can go in becoming a good tutor.

When you operate at this highest level of leadership, you must rely only on the power of attraction. Let me explain what I mean by this.

On April 22 we had St. Andrew's Day at my golf club. About 150 of us were present, including yours truly. When I arrived at the club, the other 149 did not say, "Leonard, won't you please play with me? Won't you please show me the proper stance, the proper grip, the proper swing?" They didn't do it. You know why? Because by now those fellows are aware of my incompetence as a golfer. But if you were to wave a magic wand and make of me, all of a sudden, a Sam Snead, a Ben Hogan, an Arnold Palmer, or the like, watch the picture change! Every member of that club would sit at my feet hoping to learn from me how to improve his own game. This is the power of attraction. You cannot do well at any subject without an audience automatically forming around you. Trust me on that.

If you want to be helpful to the cause of freedom in this country, seek to become a skilled expositor. If you have worked at the philosophy of freedom and an audience isn't forming, don't write and ask what the matter is. Just go back and do more of your homework.

Actually, when you get into this third level of leadership, you have to use methods that are consonant with your objective. Suppose, for instance, that my objective were your demise. I could use some fairly low-grade methods, couldn't I? But now, suppose my objective to be the making of a great poet out of you. What could I do about that? Not a thing—unless by some miracle I first learned to distinguish good poetry from bad, and then learned to impart this knowledge to you.

The philosophy of freedom is at the very pinnacle of the hierarchy of values; and if you wish to further the cause of freedom, you must use methods that are consonant with your objective. This means relying on the power of attraction.

Let me conclude with a final thought. This business of freedom is an ore that lies much deeper than most of us realize. Too many of us are prospecting wastefully on the surface. Freedom isn't something to be bought cheaply. A great effort is required to dig up this ore that will save America. And where are we to find the miners?

I think we will find these miners of the freedom-ore among those who love this country. I think we will probably find them in this room. And if you were to ask me who, in my opinion, has the greatest responsibility as a miner, I would suggest that it is the attractive individual occupying the seat you are sitting in.

Part Two

In the Market Place

One of the most important aspects of the freedom philosophy concerns its application in the market place. The matching of scarce resources against the infinite variety of human wants, the voluntary exchange of goods and services, the private ownership and control of property—all these and more are part of the economic aspect of freedom.

The role of the market economy is here examined by Benjamin Rogge, a professor of economics; Clarence Carson, a specialist in American history; and Edmund Opitz, theologian and staff member of FEE.

2

The Case for Economic Freedom

by Benjamin A. Rogge

The late Dr. Benjamin A. Rogge was Dean and Professor of Economics at Wabash College in Indiana and long a Trustee of FEE. This lecture, printed in The Freeman *in 1963, was delivered at several FEE seminars and on other occasions. It sets forth the Rogge ideal of the "unmixed" free economy.*

My economic philosophy is here offered with full knowledge that it is *not* generally accepted as the right one. On the contrary, my brand of economics has now become *Brand X,* the one that is never selected as the whitest by the housewife, the one that is said to be slow acting, the one that contains no miracle ingredient. It loses nine times out of ten in the popularity polls run on Election Day, and, in most elections, it doesn't even present a candidate.

I shall identify my brand of economics as that of economic freedom, and I shall define economic freedom as that set of economic arrangements that would exist in a society in which the government's only function would be to prevent one man from using force or fraud against another—including within this, of course, the task of national defense. So that there can be no misunderstanding here, let me say that this is pure, uncompromising *laissez-faire* economics. It is not the mixed economy; it is the unmixed economy.

I readily admit that I do not expect to see such an economy in my lifetime or in anyone's lifetime in the infinity of years ahead of us. I present it rather as the ideal we should strive for and should be disappointed in never fully attaining.

Where do we find the most powerful and persuasive case for economic freedom? I don't know; probably it hasn't been prepared as yet. Certainly it is unlikely that the case I present is the definitive one. However, it is the one that is persuasive with me, that leads me to my own deep commitment to the free market. I present it as grist for your own mill and not as the divinely inspired last word on the subject.

The Moral Case

You will note as I develop my case that I attach relatively little importance to the demonstrated efficiency of the free-market system in promoting economic growth, in raising levels of living. In fact, my central thesis is that *the most important part of the case for economic freedom is not its vaunted efficiency as a system for organizing resources, not its dramatic success in promoting economic growth, but rather its consistency with certain fundamental moral principles of life itself.*

I say, "the most important part of the case" for two reasons. First, the significance I attach to those moral principles would lead me to prefer the free enterprise system even if it were demonstrably less efficient than alternative systems, even if it were to produce a *slower* rate of economic growth than systems of central direction and control. Second, the great mass of the people of any country is never really going to understand the purely economic workings of *any* economic system, be it free enterprise or socialism. Hence, most people are going to judge an economic system by its consistency with their moral principles rather than by its purely scientific operating characteristics. If economic freedom survives in the years ahead, it will be only because a majority of the people accept its basic morality. The success of the system in bringing ever higher levels of living will be no more persuasive in the future than it has been in the past. Let me illustrate.

The doctrine of man held in general in nineteenth-century America argued that each man was ultimately responsible for what happened to him, for his own salvation, both in the here and now and in the hereafter. Thus, whether a man prospered or failed in economic life was each man's individual responsibility: each man had a right to the rewards for success and, in the same sense, deserved the punishment that came with failure. It followed as well that it is explicitly immoral to use the power of government to take from one man to give to another, to legalize Robin Hood. This doctrine of man found its economic counterpart in the system of free enterprise and, hence, the system of free enterprise was accepted and respected by many who had no real understanding of its subtleties as a technique for organizing resource use.

As this doctrine of man was replaced by one which made of man a helpless victim of his subconscious and his environment— responsible for neither his successes nor his failures—the free enterprise system came to be rejected by many who still had no real understanding of its actual operating characteristics.

Basic Values Considered

Inasmuch as my own value systems and my own assumptions about human beings are so important to the case, I want to sketch them for you.

To begin with, the central value in my choice system is individual freedom. By freedom I mean exactly and only freedom from coercion by others. I do not mean the four freedoms of President Roosevelt, which are not freedoms at all, but only rhetorical devices to persuade people to give up some of their true freedom. In the Rogge system, each man must be free to do what is his duty as he defines it, so long as he does not use force against another.

Next, I believe each man to be ultimately responsible for what happens to him. True, he is influenced by his heredity, his environment, his subconscious, and by pure chance. But I insist that precisely what makes man man is his ability to rise above these influences, to change and determine his own destiny. If this be true, then it follows that each of us is terribly and inevitably and forever responsible for everything he does. The answer to the question, "Who's to blame?" is always, "*Mea culpa,* I am."

I believe as well that man is imperfect, now and forever. He is imperfect in his knowledge of the ultimate purpose of his life, imperfect in his choice of means to serve those purposes he does select, imperfect in the integrity with which he deals with himself and those around him, imperfect in his capacity to love his fellow man. If man is imperfect, then all of his constructs must be imperfect, and the choice is always among degrees and kinds of imperfection. The New Jerusalem is never going to be realized here on earth, and the man who insists that it is, is always lost unto freedom.

Moreover, man's imperfections are intensified as he acquires the power to coerce others; "power tends to corrupt and absolute power corrupts absolutely."

This completes the listing of my assumptions, and it should be clear that the list does not constitute a total philosophy of life. Most importantly, it does not define what I believe the free man's *duty* to be, or more specifically, what I believe my own duty to be and the source of the charge to me. However important these questions, I do not consider them relevant to the choice of an economic system.

Here, then, are two sections of the case for economic freedom as I would construct it. The first section presents economic freedom as an ultimate end in itself and the second presents it as a means to the preservation of the noneconomic elements in total freedom.

Individual Freedom of Choice

The first section of the case is made in the stating of it, if one accepts the fundamental premise.

Major premise: Each man should be free to take whatever *action* he wishes, so long as he does not use force or fraud against another.

Minor premise: All economic behavior is "action" as identified above.

Conclusion: Each man should be free to take whatever action he wishes in his economic behavior, so long as he does not use force or fraud against another.

In other words, economic freedom is a part of total freedom; *if freedom is an end in itself, as our society has traditionally asserted it to be, then economic freedom is an end in itself, to be valued for itself alone and not just for its instrumental value in serving other goals.*

If this thesis is accepted, then there must always exist a tremendous presumption against each and every proposal for governmental limitation of economic freedom. What is wrong with a state system of compulsory social security? It denies to the individual his *freedom,* his right to choose what he will do with his own money resources. What is wrong with a governmentally enforced minimum wage? It denies to the employer and the employee their individual freedoms, their individual rights to enter into voluntary relationships not involving force or fraud. What is wrong with a tariff or an import quota? It denies to the individual consumer his right to buy what he wishes, wherever he wishes.

It is breathtaking to think what this simple approach would do to the apparatus of state control at all levels of government. Strike from the books all legislation that denies economic freedom to any individual, and three-fourths of all the activities now undertaken by government would be eliminated.

I am no dreamer of empty dreams, and I do not expect that the day will ever come when this principle of economic freedom as a part of total freedom will be fully accepted and applied. Yet I am convinced that unless this principle is given some standing, unless those who examine proposals for new regulation of the individual by government look on this loss of freedom as a "cost" of the proposed legislation, the chances of free enterprise surviving are small indeed. The would-be controller can always find reasons why it might seem expedient to control the individual; unless slowed down by some general feeling that it is immoral to do so, he will usually have his way.

Noneconomic Freedoms

So much for the first section of the case. Now for the second. The major premise here is the same, that is, the premise of the rightness of freedom. Here, though, the concern is with the noneconomic elements in total freedom—with freedom of speech, of religion, of the press, of personal behavior. My thesis is that these freedoms are not likely to be long preserved in a society that has denied economic freedom to its individual members.

Before developing this thesis, I wish to comment briefly on the importance of these noneconomic freedoms. I do so because we who are known as conservatives have often given too little attention to these freedoms or have even played a significant role in reducing them. The modern liberal is usually inconsistent in that he defends man's noneconomic freedoms, but is often quite indifferent to his economic freedom. The modern conservative is often inconsistent in that he defends man's economic freedom but is indifferent to his noneconomic freedoms. Why are there so few conservatives in the struggles over censorship, over denials of equality before the law for people of all races, over blue laws, and so on? Why do we let the modern liberals dominate an organization such as the American Civil Liberties Union? The general purposes of this organization are completely consistent with, even necessary to, the truly free society.

Particularly in times of stress such as these, we must fight against the general pressure to curb the rights of individual human beings, even those whose ideas and actions we detest. Now is the time to remember the example of men such as David Ricardo, the London banker and economist of the classical free-market school in the first part of the last century. Born a Jew, married to a Quaker, he devoted some part of his energy and his fortune to eliminating the legal discrimination against Catholics in the England of his day.

It is precisely because I believe these noneconomic freedoms to be so important that I believe economic freedom to be so important. The argument here could be drawn from the wisdom of the Bible and the statement that "where a man's treasure is, there will his heart be also." Give me control over a man's economic actions, and hence over his means of survival, and except for a few occasional heroes, I'll promise to deliver to you men who think and write and behave as I want them to.

The case is not difficult to make for the fully controlled economy, the true socialistic state. Milton Friedman, professor of economics at the University of Chicago, in his book, *Capitalism and Freedom*, takes the case of a socialist society that has a sincere desire to preserve the freedom of the press. The first problem would be that there would be no private capital, no private fortunes that could be used to subsidize an antisocialist, procapitalist press. Hence, the socialist state would have to do it. However, the men and women undertaking the task would have to be released from the socialist labor pool and would have to be assured that they would never be discriminated against in employment opportunities in the socialist apparatus if they were to wish to change occupations later. Then these procapitalist members of the socialist society would have to go to other functionaries of the state to secure the buildings, the presses, the paper, the skilled and unskilled workmen, and all the other components of a working newspaper. Then they would face the problem of finding distribution outlets, either creating their own (a frightening task) or using the same ones used by the official socialist propaganda organs. Finally, where would they find readers? How many men and women would risk showing up at their state-controlled jobs carrying copies of the *Daily Capitalist?*

There are so many unlikely steps in this process that the assumption that true freedom of the press could be maintained in a socialist society is so unrealistic as to be ludicrous.

Partly Socialized

Of course, we are not facing as yet a fully socialized America, but only one in which there is significant government intervention in a still predominantly private enterprise economy. Do these interventions pose any threat to the noneconomic freedoms? I believe they do.

First of all, the total of coercive devices now available to any administration of either party at the national level is so great that true freedom to work actively against the current administration (whatever it might be) is seriously reduced. For example, farmers have become captives of the government in such a way that they are forced into political alignments that seriously reduce their ability to protest actions they do not approve.

Second, the form of these interventions is such as to threaten seriously one of the real cornerstones of all freedoms—equality before the law. For example, farmers and trade union members are now encouraged and assisted in doing precisely that for which businessmen are sent to jail (i.e., acting collusively to manipulate prices). The blindfolded Goddess of Justice has been encouraged to peek, and she now says, with the jurists of the ancient regime, "First tell me who you are and then I'll tell you what your rights are." A society in which such gross inequalities before the law are encouraged in economic life is not likely to be one which preserves the principle of equality before the law generally.

We could go on to many specific illustrations. For example, the government uses its legislated monopoly to carry the mails as a means for imposing a censorship on what people send to each other in a completely voluntary relationship. A man and a woman who exchange obscene letters may not be making productive use of their time, but their correspondence is certainly no business of the government. Or to take an example from another country, Winston Churchill, as a critic of the Chamberlain government, was not permitted one minute of radio time on the government-owned and monopolized broadcasting system in the period from 1936 to the outbreak of the war he was predicting in 1939.

Each Step Leads to Another

Every act of intervention in the economic life of its citizens gives to a government additional power to shape and control the attitudes, the writings, the behavior of those citizens. Every such act is another break in the dike protecting the integrity of the individual as a free man or woman.

The free market protects the integrity of the individual by providing him with a host of decentralized alternatives rather than with one centralized opportunity. As Friedman has reminded us, even the known communist can readily find employment in capitalist America. The free market is politics-blind, religion-blind, and yes, race-blind. Do you ask about the politics or the religion of the farmer who grew the potatoes you buy at the store? Do you ask about the color of the hands that helped produce the steel you use in your office building?

South Africa provides an interesting example of this. The South Africans, of course, provide a shocking picture of racial bigotry, shocking even to a country that has its own tragic race problems. South African law clearly separates the whites from the nonwhites. Orientals have traditionally been classed as nonwhites, but South African trade with Japan has become so important in the postwar period that the government of South Africa has declared the Japanese visitors to South Africa to be officially and legally "white." The free market is one of the really great forces making for tolerance and understanding among human beings. The controlled market gives man rein to express all those blind prejudices and intolerant beliefs to which he is forever subject.

To look at this another way: The free market is often said to be impersonal, and indeed it is. Rather than a vice, this is one of its great virtues. Because the relations *are* substantially impersonal, they are not usually marked by bitter personal conflict. It is precisely because the labor union attempts to take the employment relationship *out* of the market place that bitter personal conflict so often marks union-management relationships. The intensely personal relationship is one that is civilized only by love, as between man and wife, and within the family. But man's capacity for love is severely limited by his imperfect nature. Far better, then, to economize on love, to reserve our dependence on it to those relationships where even our imperfect natures are capable of sustained action based on love. Far better, then, to build our economic system on largely impersonal relationships and on man's self-interest—a motive power with which he is generously supplied. One need only study the history of such utopian experiments as our Indiana's Harmony and New Harmony to realize that a social structure which ignores man's essential nature results in the dissension, conflict, disintegration, and dissolution of Robert Owen's New Harmony or the absolutism of Father Rapp's Harmony.

Solving the Problem of Economic Allocation

The "vulgar calculus of the market place," as its critics have described it, is still the most humane way man has yet found for solving those questions of economic allocation and division which are ubiquitous in human society. By what must seem fortunate coincidence, it is also the system most likely to produce the affluent society, to move mankind above an existence in which life is mean, nasty, brutish, and short. But, of course, this is *not* just coincidence. Under economic freedom, only man's destructive instincts are curbed by law. All of his creative instincts are released and freed to work those wonders of which free men are capable. In the controlled society only the creativity of the few at the top can be utilized, and much of this creativity must be expended in maintaining control and in fending off rivals. In the free society, the creativity of every man can be expressed—and surely by now we know that we cannot predict who will prove to be the most creative.

You may be puzzled, then, that I do not rest my case for economic freedom on its productive achievements; on its buildings, its houses, its automobiles, its bathtubs, its wonder drugs, its television sets, its sirloin steaks and green salads with Roquefort dressings. I neither feel within myself nor do I hear in the testimony of others any evidence that man's search for purpose, his longing for fulfillment, is in any significant way relieved by these accomplishments. I do not scorn these accomplishments nor do I worship them. Nor do I find in the lives of those who do worship them any evidence that they find ultimate peace and justification in their idols.

I rest my case rather on the consistency of the free market with man's essential nature, on the basic morality of its system of rewards and punishments, on the protection it gives to the integrity of the individual.

The free market cannot produce the perfect world, but it can create an environment in which each imperfect man may conduct his lifelong search for purpose in his own way, in which each day he may order his life according to his own imperfect vision of his destiny, suffering both the agonies of his errors and the sweet pleasure of his successes. This freedom is what it means to be a man; this is the God-head, if you wish.

I give you, then, the free market, the expression of man's economic freedom and the guarantor of all his other freedoms.

3

Free Enterprise: The Key to Prosperity

by Clarence B. Carson

Dr. Carson is an experienced observer and analyst of political and economic affairs. He is a specialist in American history with his Ph.D. degree from Vanderbilt University. He is the author of several books, including a five-volume text, A Basic History of the United States.

The copyright to this article is held by Clarence B. Carson.

Free enterprise is widely acclaimed in the United States. Politicians, generally, declare in favor of it; editorialists frequently laud it; Chambers of Commerce have writing contests about it; even automobile stickers praise its virtues. Yet much of our enterprise is restrained, restricted, hampered, regulated, controlled, or prohibited. As an old saw has it, "What you do speaks so loud I can't hear what you are saying." By our practice, we say that we believe in free enterprise—*except . . .* Except for public utilities. Except for the railroads. Except for mail delivery. Except for medical services. Except for housing, financing, and real estate transactions. Except for large corporations. Except for education. Except for interest rates. Except for farmers. Except for small business. Except for industrial workers. In short, a case could be made that Americans believe in free enterprise except in whatever activities they happen to be considering.

It may be helpful, then, to consider free enterprise in terms of itself, minus all the partisan exceptions. The approach here will be to pose five questions: What is free enterprise? What are the objections to free enterprise? How may the objections be answered? What are the practical advantages of free enterprise? Is free enterprise necessary to freedom? The answers to these should provide some perspective on free enterprise.

What Is Free Enterprise?

Free enterprise is a way of going about meeting our needs and wants by providing for ourselves or by freely entering into transactions with others. The opposite of free enterprise is hampered, restricted, controlled, or prohibited enterprise. The enterprise itself must be conducted in an orderly fashion within the framework of rules, but if the rules inhibit entry or hamper activity they become restrictions on enterprise. It is clear enough, for example, that traffic at an intersection must be regulated in its flow but that reasonable rules promote rather than inhibit the effective use of the street. On the other hand, if a city made a rule that taxicabs were to be limited to those presently in operation it would be equally clear that enterprise was being hampered. In a similar fashion, if a city adopted a rule forbidding any taxi to use the streets within its boundaries, that type of enterprise would be prohibited. Thus, government may be an adjunct or an obstacle to enterprise.

Free enterprise does not exist in a vacuum; it must be institutionally supported and protected. One of these institutions is *government*. Government is necessary to prohibit and punish the private violation of the rights of those who peacefully use their energies and resources in a productive way. Government is necessary also to punish fraud and deception, to settle disputes which may arise, and to regulate the use of public facilities such as highways. Another basic institution for free enterprise is *private property*. For enterprise to be free, those who engage in it must be free; that entails having property in themselves and what they produce. Enterprisers must have title to their goods in order either to consume them or to trade with others. Real property in land and buildings is essential to have a place to produce and to market goods and services. Private property not only supplies opportunities for the individual to provide for himself but it also places inherent limits on his activity. He can only rightfully sell and convey to another what is his in the first place. Private property also sets bounds to enterprise by restricting the owner to the use of what is his own or to that which the rightful owner authorizes others to use.

A third ingredient of free enterprise is *free access to the market.* A market is any arena within which buyers and sellers meet to effect their transactions. Under free enterprise neither buyer nor seller is prevented from making transactions by government decree or private threats or use of force.

The motor of free enterprise, indeed, of all enterprise, is *individual initiative.* Individuals provide the energy for the making of goods and providing of services. They conceive, invent, design, engineer, produce, and market goods through their endeavor. The great spur to produce is the increase of one's goods or the profit he may make by selling them. Here again, the importance of private property and free access to the market may be seen. If men cannot keep as property what they produce, if they cannot market it, their incentive to produce is lessened or removed.

The great regulator of free enterprise is *competition.* Competition among sellers keeps prices down and tends to assure that the customer will be served. Competition among buyers provides a market in which those goods that are wanted can be sold at a profit. Prices are the result of this competition. Although any owner may offer his wares at a price acceptable to him, he can only sell when he has found a buyer willing to pay his price.

What Are the Objections to Free Enterprise?

There is no doing without human enterprise, for without it we would all be impoverished and our survival in doubt. The main question we have in regard to it is whether it shall be free or hampered. Reformist and revolutionary intellectuals have launched a massive assault over the past century against the market, private property, the profit motive, and other facets of free enterprise. The thrust of their efforts has been to discover fatal flaws in the system, which they usually describe as capitalist, and to propose that government either supervise or take over the operation of the economy. They can be classified in one of two broad categories: *meliorism* or *socialism.*

Meliorism is the view that what is wrong with free enterprise can be *corrected by government intervention.* It holds that government can control, restrict, limit, regulate, tax, and redistribute so as to better the lot of the people and avoid the worst difficulties which they believe are inherent in free enterprise. Meliorists are hardly enthusiastic about private property and individual enterprise, but they do not usually attack them head on.

Socialists do directly attack property, private enterprise, the profit system, and what they call capitalism. They propose to abolish them with governmental (or collective or public) ownership of the means of production of goods. Socialism divides roughly into two camps: *democratic socialism* and *communism*. Democratic socialists are distinguished by a gradual approach to socialism because they are tied to popular elections and must move as the electorate will. Communists are revolutionaries who move toward socialism swiftly and by drastic measures once they come to power. They are characterized by one-party rule, and by totalitarian control over the lives of the people.

While socialists and meliorists have a barrage of objections to free enterprise, the following points are central to their argument.

One of their arguments which has broad appeal is that *free enterprise produces cutthroat competition,* often described as dog eat dog, or rugged individualism. The charge is that some people compete so vigorously that they drive competitors out of business or buy them out. While this is made to sound as if it were a special variety of competition, it is really a plea for government intervention to limit and restrain competition.

Competition as War

A related objection to free enterprise is that *competition amounts to industrial warfare,* that it pits men against one another in the quest for material possessions. Those who advance this notion say that free enterprise depends upon and calls forth the baser human motives, that it is materialistic, that it makes selfishness into a virtue, and that it fosters competition rather than leading men to cooperate with one another. This conception of competition as war has served over the years as the major propellant of government intervention by way of antitrust legislation, fair trade laws, and other regulatory measures.

An objection heard frequently is that *the consumer is taken advantage of and deceived* by advertising and a great variety of marginally different products and services. According to John Kenneth Galbraith in *The Affluent Society,* all kinds of frills are produced which people do not really need but are induced to buy by advertising. Ralph Nader has made a career out of protecting customers from themselves. The thrust of the consumer protection movement has been to try to replace the ancient rule of letting the buyer beware with government prescriptions about how goods may be sold.

Although those who raise objections to free enterprise are often ambiguous about the merits of free enterprise, one of their objections is that under this system there is *imperfect competition.* This is the charge that businesses do not compete with one another with sufficient vigor. Instead, they say, companies engaged in the same business conspire with one another to raise prices. Or, as a result of competition, one company drives all others out and proceeds to charge what the traffic will bear.

In the middle of the nineteenth century, Karl Marx claimed that in industrial capitalist countries there was a trend toward monopoly where a single company would dominate a whole industry. Indeed, he held that large companies would grow larger until they had a whole industry under their sway. This argument crops up again and again in many different guises. The term "oligopoly" was devised to describe the situation when several giants control an industry. The thrust of these arguments in the United States has been to press for breaking up large concentrations of industry.

Some objectors to free enterprise hold that one of its least desirable traits is that it results in *unequal distribution* of goods and services. The most commonly repeated phrase is that the rich get richer and the poor get poorer. Many lack the bare necessities, while others have more than anyone could consume or use. Those who make these charges against free enterprise may not believe that goods should be exactly equally distributed, but they do argue that everyone should have enough, at the least, to meet their basic needs.

Probably, the most devastating charge against the free enterprise system is that it is responsible for the *business cycle.* Business activity does apparently go in cycles, with periods of prosperity alternating with recessions and depressions. The most common claim of reformists is that businessmen claim too large a share of the proceeds from their products, that there is a resulting decline in consumer demand, leading to recession or depression. The way to prevent this, they say, is for government to soak up the excess in taxes and distribute the wealth more or less directly to those who will spend it for consumer goods.

How May Objections to Free Enterprise be Answered?

Many of the objections to free enterprise arise either from misinformation about economics or the hope that somehow the requirements of economy can be evaded—itself a misconception regarding economics. One of the best ways to answer them, then, is to call up some of the basic principles of economics.

Economics has to do with scarcity. The character of economics is indicated by the conventional uses of words related to it. For example, one dictionary defines "economical" as "avoiding waste or extravagance; thrifty." It "implies prudent planning in the disposition of resources so as to avoid unnecessary waste. . . ." "Economy" refers to "thrifty management; frugality in the expenditure or consumption of money, materials, etc." Economics can be defined as the study of the most effective means for persons to maintain and increase the supply of goods and services at their disposal. Goods and services are understood to be scarce, and economics has to do with the frugal management of time, energy, resources, and materials so as to bring about the greatest increase in the supply of goods and services most desired.

There is every reason to believe that man is naturally inclined to use as little energy and materials to produce as many goods as he can from them. In short, he is predisposed to be economical. If this were not the case, it is easy to believe that he would long since have perished from the face of the earth. But this economic penchant gives rise to a problem rather than resolving all problems. There are two ways for an individual to augment the supply of goods and services at his disposal. (1) He can provide them for himself. (2) He can acquire them from others. Again, there are two ways for an individual to acquire them from others. (1) He can acquire them by exchange (in which we may well include free gifts). Or (2) he can take them from someone who possesses them.

It is this latter option that raises hob in determining what is economic. Strictly speaking, robbery could be quite economical for an individual. By stealing, an individual can greatly increase the supply of goods and services available to him with only a very little expenditure of energy and materials. A bank robber may, for example, spend half an hour using a twenty-dollar gun and enrich himself, say, to the extent of $20,000.

That might indeed be economical for an individual, but it is not so for society at large. Economics has to do with the increase of the supply of goods in general, not just the individual's gain. The bank robber augments his personal supply at the expense of those from whom he has stolen. Moreover, he may reduce the general supply further by the threat he poses to trade and the loss of incentive men have to produce when they are uncertain that they will be able to keep the rewards of their efforts. For these reasons, theft should not be considered economical.

Even so, the example of the bank robber is not frivolous. All redistribution schemes are proposals to use force to take from those who have and give to those who have not. If governments do such things, it is still theft, albeit *legal* theft. And its effect on the general supply would reasonably be the same as any other kind of theft.

The Problem of Scarcity

The economic question, then, is under what system is the supply of goods most apt to be replenished and increased? Is it one in which there is free access to the market, in which men receive the fruits of their labor for their own use or disposal, in which individual initiative is fully brought into play, and in which sellers and buyers are in competition? Or is it one in which access is controlled, in which property is controlled by government or held in common, in which individual initiative is discouraged, and in which competition is restrained? If we understand that the basic problem is scarcity, these are the questions about enterprise that need to be answered. The problem is really one of production, and with that in mind the objections to free enterprise discussed earlier can now be answered.

The attack on competition, because of the rigors involved in it and because there are losers, is really an attack on effective pro-duction. Such attacks gain widespread support quite often because of the desire to avoid the requirements of competition. Anyone can see the advantage of competition when it is among others. After all, competition brings down prices, increases the variety and quality of goods, and increases demand as well as supply. But competition is not nearly so attractive when we have to engage in it, especially once we have made our mark in production. It is not only necessary to get there by competition but also to stay there by changing and improving products, offering superior service, and the like. The argument against cutthroat competition is really not an argument against free enterprise but an argument against having to compete by those who have jobs, have arrived at a position, and want to retain it without further competition. When government restricts entry to any field, it is the "have-nots" who are most apt to be kept out. The main opportunity for men to improve their condition is by way of free access to the market. Free enterprise offers ready entry to all comers and provides what assurance there can be for continued replenishing of goods.

Cooperation and Competition

Competition is not a kind of warfare. To the extent that it pits men against one another it does so by stimulating them to excel. When each man is doing his best all may benefit: those who participate by producing and excelling, the rest of society by what is produced. There are no necessary victims in competition. Of course, not everyone can excel or even compete at the same level. But any man is a winner who discovers that way and level at which he can effectively produce and serve. Most people cannot run the four-minute mile. That does not mean that we put weights on the faster racers in order to enable the slower runners to keep up. People do well to compete at their own levels of ability.

Competition does not prevent or even downgrade cooperation, either. Under free enterprise people must and do cooperate in many ways to provide us with the amenities of life. Industrial production today requires cooperation of a very high degree. The assembly line is the epitome of organized cooperation. The making and selling of automobiles, for example, requires the cooperation of all sorts of entrepreneurs, financiers, service providers, manufacturers, assembly line workers, transportation workers, designers, engineers, and mechanics.

On a less grandiose scale, we usually take for granted that any one of a hundred items will be available when we want it. I may decide, for example, that I need a new box of pencils. I go to the nearest store which carries sundries and discover that the store not only has pencils but a considerable variety of them as well. How did this happen? Did the store know that I was about out of pencils and that they should stock some in case I should come by? Not at all, yet a lot of foresight had gone into providing them for my convenience. Not only had companies brought together in factories those who could make pencils but also the need had been predicted, the capital set aside for producing them, supplies ordered, raw material prepared, and the pencils produced and placed by wholesalers with my local store. True, businesses in direct competition with one another may not do a great deal of cooperating with one another, but that may be largely because of the antitrust laws.

The extensive nature of competition is not generally well understood, and certainly not by most who write about imperfect competition. Most critics talk of competition as if it involved only direct competition among the suppliers of a particular kind of product. That kind of competition is only the tip of the iceberg of competition. For example, if General Motors were the only maker of automobiles in the United States, there would still be competition. The Chevrolet division would still be competing with Pontiac, Pontiac with Buick, Buick with Oldsmobile, these with Cadillac, and all of them with foreign imports.

Varieties of Competition

But competition is much broader and more varied than the above example would suggest. New cars are in competition with used ones. Automobiles, as a means of transportation, are in competition with busses, airlines, trains, motorcycles, trucks, bicycles, horses, and walking. Further, human wants are extensive, and the means for satisfying them are numerous and diverse. Instead of buying a car, or a second one, a given consumer may choose to add a room on his house, buy a boat, equip his family room with an amusement center, put his money in savings, or what not—all because he judged the car he might have bought too expensive. That kind of choice crops up in whatever direction we look.

The number of foods which will sustain life, either singly or in combination with others, can hardly be counted. There are many fibers, natural and artificial, from which to make clothes, all sorts of building materials, a considerable number of fuels, to give a few examples. If the price of any one of these is raised significantly, or the quality declines, alternative means are likely to be found to gratify the want. If oranges become more expensive, apples may be substituted. Competition may not be as broad as the range of commodities on the market, but we come nearer to the truth when we view it that way than when we attempt to confine it to the makers of a single commodity.

Access to the Market

Imperfect competition, rightly understood, is a condition which exists when access to the market is hampered by legal restrictions or the use or threat of force. Otherwise, the extent of competition may be presumed to be adequate in the market, else new companies could be expected to enter the field. Whether competition is adequate or not cannot be determined by counting the number of companies engaged in making a commodity, by comparing the shares of the market which companies have, by calculating their costs and comparing them with retail prices, or any other such empirical device. The effectiveness of competition can only be measured to the extent that consumer satisfaction with the goods offered him in the market can be measured. When there is free access to the market, anyone who believes that there is some unmet want is free to enter the market and supply it. It happens all the time.

The critics are right when they say that under free enterprise goods are not equally distributed among the populace. Where there is private property, not everyone has the same amount of property. If such equality could exist, it would depend upon distributing everything equally and then stopping all transactions or change at that point. It would have to mean, also, the stopping of all births and deaths, for as soon as an imbalance between births and deaths occurred, a new inequality would either exist or an entire redistribution have to take place. But before such a new distribution could be completed the situation would no doubt have changed again and the effort to establish equality failed.

This is by way of saying that equality in the distribution of goods cannot be. In no extensive society has there ever been equality of possessions; everywhere and always there has been disparity. The present writer does not know of a single family, which is surely the smallest social unit, in which each has exactly the same amount of possessions as every other, nor can he readily visualize how it could happen. Give two small children each a toy. One will have his torn up within the hour, while the other may keep his in good repair for months or years. It is so for adults as well; some manage well, work hard, take care of what they have received, others hardly at all. The basic question for an economy and society is not one of the disparity of wealth but of the justice of the arrangement under which it is acquired and maintained.

Market Success

What is a just distribution of goods and services? Given the differences in talent, tenacity, prudence, and willingness to work, it is surely not justice to distribute goods on the basis of equality, or even need. Under the free enterprise system men are understood to have got what they deserved when they get as property what they have produced and get in exchange for it what the highest bidder in the market is willing to pay. Does that mean that the case of the have-nots is hopeless under free enterprise? Not at all, for free enterprise offers them the best opportunity there is for improving their condition. When there are no obstacles in the way of entering any endeavor, men can and do change from have-nots to haves. There are many historical examples of men who have started with nothing and even attained great wealth. There are many more examples of those who have started with little and attained a competence.

There is much evidence to show that it is government activity, not free enterprise, which is responsible for the so-called business cycle. The cyclical change from prosperity to depression-recession to prosperity can be corollated with increases and decreases in the supply of money. Dramatic increases in the money supply result in expansive business activity and tend to create a boom atmosphere. When the supply of money is decreased or stabilized, activity slows, and recessions follow. If there is a severe deflation, such as the one that followed the stock market crash in 1929, a deep depression can be the result. In precise terms, the cycles result from credit expansions and contractions. The villain of the piece is government manipulation of the money supply by way of the Federal Reserve system. The cure lies not in government intervention to hamper enterprise, but in a sound money that cannot be manipulated.

What Are the Practical Advantages of Free Enterprise?

It is not necessary to rely on theory alone to determine the superiority of free enterprise over other methods in providing for people's needs. There is historical evidence that when enterprise is freed from the restrictive hand of government and when property is rigorously protected, production increases along with general economic well-being. It needs to be understood, however, that much of economic history is a record of government interventions and restraints and that there are always some. Consequently, restriction is usually a matter of degree, not of absolutes. Nonetheless, there have been periods in the life of nations when enterprise has been freed from many of the restraints, and these provide favorable evidence for free enterprise.

England in the nineteenth century is a striking example of what can happen when enterprise is freed. In the early 1700s there were still numerous restrictions and special privileges hampering enterprise in that land. Beginning in 1689, however, the British made almost continuous progress in the direction of freer enterprise. By the 1820s, enterprise was substantially free in Great Britain, though the movement for free trade is usually thought of as culminating with the repeal of the Corn Laws in 1846. It is worth noting, too, that this freeing of enterprise was accompanied by the general establishment of widespread liberty, the limiting of the monarch, the toleration in religion, and protections of speech and of the press. These things go hand in hand.

The economic results were not long in coming. It has been estimated that England's industrial output increased tenfold between 1820 and 1913. Coal production was approximately 10 million tons in 1800, 44 million tons in 1850, and 154 million tons in 1880. Iron production was about 17,000 tons in 1740. By

1840 it had reached 1,390,000 tons, and a few years later had nearly tripled from that. Population increase did not quite keep up with industrial production, but there was unprecedented population growth as well. By the end of the nineteenth century, Englishmen were generally better off materially than ever before in history.

When Enterprise Is Freed

To show Britain's place of leadership in the world, however, it is necessary to compare British economic achievement with that of other leading countries. Great Britain's percentage of manufacturing production in the world was 31.8 in 1870. By comparison, that of the United States was 23.3, that of Germany 13.2, and that of France 10.3 among the leading countries. In 1860, Britain had 23 per cent of the world trade, compared with 11 per cent for France and 9 per cent for the United States. In 1880, Britain had more than $6\frac{1}{2}$ million tons of shipping, compared to less than $1\frac{1}{2}$ million for the United States, the nearest competitor.

The nineteenth century was in many ways a kind of Golden Age. There was a quickening of activity in many nations, and England was surely the center from which so many improvements radiated outward to the rest of the world. The symbol of England's greatness was the Royal Navy, but the wonders were much more the achievements of the merchant marine. The ships that plied the seas from their home base in the tight little isle carried not only the abounding goods of a productive nation but also statesmen, ideas, and men confident in the superiority of their institutions eager to teach others the arts of peace. The difference between England and many other lands was the stability of her institutions and the freedom of her enterprise.

In many ways, the emergence of the United States in the early twentieth century as the leading manufacturing and agricultural producer was even more remarkable than the nineteenth-century achievement of Britain. After all, Britain had had several centuries of fairly steady advance on the world stage before the nineteenth century. What became the United States, by contrast, had been a colony until the late eighteenth century and had only emerged as a nation to be respected by European nations in the course of the nineteenth century. Yet in less than a century of independence, the United States was thrusting toward leadership among the producing peoples in the world. The country had been crisscrossed with railroads; the wilderness had been tamed, and the great Mississippi basin had become one of the most productive areas in the world. The political institutions of the United States had been designed from the outset to restrain and limit government. The energies of men were largely released in peaceful pursuits, and the people achieved wonders of building, invention, and development of manufacturing, transportation, and farming.

The Destruction of Enterprise

Examples of the repressive effect of government on enterprise are even more plentiful, but it will be possible here to give only one example. Appropriately, the example chosen will be Britain, since the focus has been upon that land in the freeing of enterprise. In the early years of the twentieth century, the British government began to clamp down on enterprise, in what one historian has called *The Strange Death of Liberal England*. The impact of this on the British was being felt as a general decline by the 1930s, but the assault on enterprise did not reach its peak until after World War II.

In 1945, a Labour Party came to power in England committed to enacting the socialist programs it had long been advancing. The party did so with great haste, and in short order the Labourites completed the wreck of what remained of a once vigorous and healthy economy. The economy had suffered greatly from the interventions of the interwar years. It was hampered even more drastically by wartime restrictions. But the measures of the Labour government came close to banishing private economy from the land.

The wreckage was wrought by nationalization, controls, regulations, high taxes, and compulsory provision of services. There was a concerted effort to plan for and control virtually all economic activity in the land. The initiative for action was taken from the people and vested in a bureaucracy. Where industries were taken over, they were placed under the authority of boards which were in no position to act responsibly.

Equal Distinction and Having Less

English socialists had long been committed to as near equal distribution of goods and services as they could. Therefore, the Labour government undertook redistribution with a right good will. They levied steeply graduated income taxes, taxed "luxury" goods at high rates, controlled prices of food, clothing, and shelter, and rationed many items that were in particularly short supply. They provided free medical services, gave pensions, and otherwise aided those with little or no earned incomes. They distributed and they distributed.

The more they distributed, the less they had to distribute. Not only did such shortages as they had known during war continue, but others cropped up as well. One writer says, "By 1948, rations had fallen well below the wartime average. In one week, the average man's allowance was thirteen ounces of meat, one and a half ounces of cheese, six ounces of butter and margarine, one ounce of cooking fat, eight ounces of sugar, two pints of milk, and one egg." Even bread, which had *not* been rationed during the war, was rationed beginning in 1946. The government had first attempted to fool the English people into buying less bread by reducing the amount in a loaf. When that did not work, they turned to rationing. Housing, clothing, food, fuel—everything, it seemed—was in short supply.

By the summer of 1947, the British government was making no secret of its problem. The country was inundated with government posters, proclaiming "We Work or Want," posters whose threat was all bark and no bite. The fact is that when production is separated from distribution to any considerable extent the incentives to produce are reduced. When this is accompanied by numerous restrictions and loss of private control over property (as it was in England)—restrictions which hamper people in their productive efforts—goods and services will be in ever shorter supply.

Since that time, Britain has off and on, but slowly, reduced the extent to which it restricts so as to hamper industry. Democratic socialists in many lands have lost some of their enthusiasm for nationalizing property and have favored government control with largely private ownership, as has been the case in Sweden. The

United States in recent years has removed or reduced some of its regulations, though the central features of the Welfare State remain. Communists remain unmoved by all evidence, continue to thrust for government ownership of all productive property, and cause untold suffering with their drastic measures against private enterprise wherever they come to power. The most recent dramatic instance occurred in Ethiopia, with its hunger and starvation.

But whatever rulers have or have not learned from their determined efforts to establish roadblocks to enterprise, one thing appears universally to have eluded them. It is this: They still have not grasped that men must be in control of their own affairs if their enterprising spirit is to be unleashed in constructive efforts. For this, they must have the full measure of freedom, not that portion which politicians prate about as "human rights," thus ignoring or shunting aside the rights to property.

Is Free Enterprise Essential to Freedom?

Freedom is a seamless cloth, its parts inseparable from one another. Free enterprise is a part of and necessary to freedom within a society. It not only provides bread better than any other system but it also buttresses and rounds out the structure of political, social, intellectual, and religious freedom of a people.

Freedom is indivisible. Some of those who profess to value freedom but not free enterprise have tried to maintain that this is not the case. They distinguish between property rights and human rights, and hold that human rights are superior to property rights. Property rights are, however, human rights, rights of humans to the fruits of their labor. Arguments about which rights are superior are on the same order of those as to whether the heart is superior to the liver or whether the lungs are superior to the kidneys, for the fact is that human life and activity depend on all of these. Just so, freedom depends on the right to property just as it does to rights of free speech.

The reason for this needs to be explored. There is no human activity that does not involve the use of property. We cannot sleep, wake, eat, walk, drive, fly, swim, boat, work, go to church, print a paper, view a movie, make a speech, procreate, or engage in conversation without using property in some one or more of its dimensions. If a church cannot be owned by its communicants, their freedom to worship is under the control of someone else. If a press cannot be privately owned, freedom of the press is an illusion. If government controls all property, freedom of speech is something belonging to government, not to individuals.

The Breadth of Freedom

Free enterprise—which embraces private property—does not mean simply the right to engage in material production and distribution. It means the right to engage in every kind of productive activity: not only the manufacture of widgets but also forming a fraternal organization, starting a charitable organization, publishing a newspaper, organizing a church, and founding a college. Not all undertakings involve profit making, but all do involve the use of property and the making of transactions.

The thrust of government intervention in the economy is toward government control of all life and the destruction of the independence of the citizenry. Not every government intervention will in fact result in the totalizing of intervention, of course. Government may intervene here and not there, may extend its power for a time and withdraw, may even reverse its direction. But the tendency of men in power is to grasp for more. The tendency of those who gain some control over enterprise is to extend it into more and more areas.

Many Western socialists do not accept the totalitarian tendency of their doctrines. They cling to the belief that freedom can be retained in areas that they consider valuable while it is yielded up in the economic realm. They have nowhere, to my knowledge, submitted their theory to the test. Their experiments with socialism have been limited. They have nationalized *some* industries, expropriated *some* property, taken over the providing of *some* services, created bureaucracies to control *some* undertakings, empowered labor unions, and drawn up various sorts of restrictions. They have usually allowed considerable enterprise within the interstices of their systems. Such systems are oppressive, do hamper enterprise, do not function very well, but they are not totalitarian—not yet, anyway. They are not full-fledged socialism, either.

The same cannot be said for those countries in which there have been all-out efforts to abolish private property, to control every aspect of the economy, to bring all employment under state control, in a word to institute socialism in its most virulent form, Communism. In these countries, freedom is crushed. Such a country is ruled by terror, the terror administered by secret police, by the shot in the back of the neck, by slave labor camps, by the arbitrariness of all government action, which is the ultimate terror. Terror is as essential to thoroughgoing socialism as sunlight is to photosynthesis. It is essential because man naturally has to look after himself and seeks means to do so, turns whatever he has into private property, and exerts his imagination and enterprise to provide for himself and his own. Man forever labors to carve out areas of freedom for himself. By so doing, he subverts socialist control. The only means for holding him back is terror and arbitrary government control.

Those who favor free enterprise are working to maintain or establish human freedom. They are on the side of the human spirit wherever efforts are being made to crush it. Those who stand for free enterprise have a noble cause, for it is the cause of freedom and of free men.

4

The American Way in Economics

by Edmund A. Opitz

The Reverend Mr. Opitz is a member of the staff of the Foundation for Economic Education, book review editor of The Freeman, *lecturer, and seminar discussion leader.*

In this article from the October 1964 Freeman *he shows how the free market economy will spring naturally from the proper spiritual and constitutional framework.*

E conomics deals with our daily bread, with the provisioning of our material and creaturely needs, with the way we make our living. But the way a person makes his living is related to the things he is living for; and a nation's mode of operating in the economic realm cannot be detached from that nation's understanding of the end and purpose of human life. An economic system, in other words, functions within a framework of ethical and spiritual components. It has a legal framework, also. This means that the discussion of economic concepts cannot proceed very far without invoking spiritual and constitutional concepts.

If we look back over our own history, in its religious, political, and economic sectors, we note that one key word fits each of them. The key word is "Freedom." I am willing to grant that the motives of the Pilgrims and the Puritans were mixed. But ask yourself this question: "If the Separatists had been able to worship God as they pleased, without hindrance or penalty, in England, would they have emigrated to this continent when they did—or at all?" Merely to ask this question is to get the obvious answer: The impelling motive behind the seventeenth-century migrations and resettlements was the search for a place where these religious dissenters might be free to worship God as they chose. Writing about the men and women who established Plymouth colony, Alexis de Tocqueville said, ". . . it was a purely intellectual craving that called them from the comforts of their former homes; and in facing the inevitable sufferings of exile their object was the triumph of an idea."

It was the idea of human freedom under God. Now, candor compels us to admit that the Puritan idea of freedom contained some blind spots. The Dissenters sought freedom on these shores to worship God as *they* pleased; it was not their aim to establish the general condition of religious liberty where every man might worship after his own fashion. In the political realm they countenanced governmental invasions of personal liberty which we would regard today as intolerable; and in the economic sector their practices could hardly be described as free market. But despite their shortcomings in practice, these people had hold of an idea which had the power to act as a solvent of existing injustices, taboos, and ignorance. This dynamic idea was the principle of liberty. It could hardly have been otherwise, for the Puritans were children of the Reformation, and the spiritual liberty stressed by the Reformers could not help branching out into secular liberties.

A Great Religious Tradition

Let's listen to the words of Edmund Burke on this point. Burke made a great speech on conciliation with the American colonies and warned his hearers that the colonists were made of stern stuff. The way they all share "in their ordinary governments," he writes, "never fails to inspire them with lofty sentiments. . . . If anything were wanting to this necessary operation of the form of government, religion would have given it a complete effect. Religion, always a principle of energy, in this new people is no way worn out or impaired; and their mode of professing it is also one main cause of this free spirit. The people are Protestants, and of that kind which is the most adverse to all implicit submission of mind and opinion. This is a persuasion not only favorable to liberty, but built upon it. . . . The dissenting interests have sprung up in direct opposition to all the ordinary powers of the world, and could justify that opposition only on a strong claim to natural liberty. Their very existence depended on the powerful and unremitted assertion of that claim. All Protestantism, even the most cold and passive, is a sort of dissent. But the religion most prevalent in our northern colonies is a refinement on the principle of resistance; it is the dissidence of dissent, and the protestantism of the Protestant religion."

The Founding Fathers, in other words, were the inheritors of a great religious tradition and the American dream of a society of free men was largely a projection of that religion. This is how the original American equation got its built-in religious dimension.

Christian by Absorption

Every society is held together because its members share a common understanding of certain basic principles. There must be a consensus as to the object of ultimate concern—God. There must be some agreement as to the relation between God and man, and as to the nature of man and his proper end. There must be some agreement as to what constitutes justice, honor, and virtue. The source from which a society derives its understanding of these matters is its religion. In this sense, every society is cradled in some religion, Christian or otherwise. The culture of China is unthinkable without Confucianism; Indian society is the expression of Hinduism; and Islam is composed of followers of Mohammed.

In like fashion, our Western culture stems from the Judeo-Christian tradition; we are a branch of Christendom. As one of our editorial writers has said, "The United States is not Christian in any formal sense, its churches are not full on Sundays, and its citizens transgress the precepts freely. But it is Christian in the sense of absorption. The basic teachings of Christianity are in its bloodstream. The central doctrine of its political system—the inviolability of the individual—is the doctrine inherited from 1900 years of Christian insistence upon the immortality of the soul. Christian idealism is manifest in the culture and habits of the people. . . . The American owes all this to the Church . . . He owes it to the leadership the Church provided in the founding, settlement, and political integration of his incredibly bounteous land." (*Fortune*, January, 1940)

In short, our institutions and our way of life are intimately related to the basic dogmas of the Christian religion. From this faith we derive our notions of the meaning of life, the moral order, the dignity of persons, and the rights and responsibilities of individuals. Ours is a Christian society, with its counterpart in a secular political state.

And this religious heritage, to put the matter briefly, spells out into personal liberty in the political and social spheres. The God who gave us the freedom to accept or reject Him certainly intends us to be free in our relations with other men. People who believe this will, when they come to draft the fundamental rules for the governing of a society, design a political structure severely limited in scope. They will limit government so as to unshackle the productive and creative energies of men. Government will keep the peace by restraining those who disturb it.

The men who drafted the Constitution did not design a stream-lined political structure. James Madison and the others had been once burnt by government, and they were twice shy. They created a political structure in which the national government was to be internally self-governed by three separate but balanced powers, and the several states were to retain their original sovereignty in order to act as a counterpoise to the central authority. This entire political equilibrium revolved around the sovereign individual; the only excuse for government was to secure him in his rights. The Founding Fathers knew that a free government implies an unfree people, so in the interests of personal liberty they pinned down their government to strictly limited, defined, and delegated functions. The words "no" and "not" employed in restraint of governmental power occur 24 times in the first seven articles of the Constitution and 22 more times in the Bill of Rights.

The Realm of Economics

So far, I have had little to say about economics, as such. The omission is deliberate, and the reason is this: An economic system does not have to be constructed; establish the proper spiritual and constitutional framework and an economic order will construct itself. In this respect, an economic order is somewhat analogous to a crystal. Not even the most skilled chemist could build up a crystal by adding molecule to molecule; but almost anyone can set up the conditions under which a crystal will construct itself.

Remember how you made rock candy, by preparing a saturated sugar solution, and then dipping into this clear thick liquid a piece of string on which the sugar crystals formed? Something of this sort happens in human affairs in the realm of economics, but to understand this we'll have to examine the nature of economic activity and the human purposes this serves.

Economics is the realm of business, industry, and trade. On the surface, economics deals with prices, production, exchange, and the operations of the market place as a reflection of our buying and consuming habits. Fundamentally, however, economics is concerned with the conservation and stewardship of the earth's scarce goods. At the basic level, there are four such goods. One is human energy. A man can put forth just so much work before exhaustion demands rest and repair for his body, and as a result men devise labor-saving devices. A second scarce good is time— the thing that's always running out on us. A third is material resources—iron ore, wood pulp, living space, and so on. The fourth is natural energy, such as is found in a waterfall. These goods-in-short-supply are our birthright as creatures of this planet. Use them wisely, as natural piety dictates and common sense confirms—that is, providently and economically—and human well-being results.

As a result of economic activity, using and combining these four scarce goods, we get the bewildering variety of goods in today's markets—houses, automobiles, foodstuffs, entertainment, dental services, round-the-world trips and so on. Relative to the demand for these things, they are scarce—else they wouldn't be economic goods! Every day we are faced with the necessity of choosing between two or more things we want, knowing that if we buy this we must do without that. We work at some job or other, and are paid for our efforts, which enables us to buy things to satisfy our most urgent wants. The net result of this kind of individual action in society is that scarce goods are allocated efficiently.

Economic activity in a healthy society is in the realm of means, being somewhat analogous to digestion in a healthy individual. A person has aims for his life which far transcend the processes by which his body is maintained; but if these processes begin to falter and work badly, his attention is drawn away from his life's goal and begins to focus on them instead. He becomes a hypochondriac. Given other circumstances he may become a glutton. In any event, he has idolatrously erected means into ends, to the detriment of both means and ends.

Economic activity, too, may become an end in itself for a person whose life lacks more worthwhile goals, or even for a society when its value system is scrambled. It is up to a society's religious institutions to keep its value system in repair; and if they fail to respond with new duties to meet new occasions, it is inevitable that the false gods will take over. Then we may have what Albert Jay Nock decried as "economism"—the doctrine that the whole of life consists in the production, exchange, and consumption of things.

Beyond Basic Needs

All creatures take the world pretty much as they find it, except man. Man alone has the gifts which enable him to entertain an idea and then transform his environment in accordance with it. He is equipped with needs which the world as it is cannot satisfy. Thus he is compelled to alter and rearrange the natural order by employing his energy on raw materials so as to put them into consumable form. Before he can do much of anything else, man must manufacture, grow, and transport. His creaturely needs man shares with the animals, but he alone employs economic means— tools and capital—to satisfy them. This is an enormous leap upward, for by relying on the economic means man becomes so efficient at satisfying his bodily hungers that he gains a measure of independence from them. When they are assuaged, he feels the tug of hungers no animal ever feels: for truth, for beauty, for meaning, for God.

It conveys something like a half truth and a whole error to label man a spiritual being. He is, in fact, a spiritual being who eats, feels the cold, and needs shelter. Whatever may be man's capacities in the upper reaches of his nature—to think, dream, pray, create— it is certain that he will attain to none of these unless he survives. And he cannot survive for long unless he engages in economic activity. At the lowest level economic action achieves merely economic ends: food, clothing, and shelter. But when these matters are efficiently in hand, economic action is a means to all our ends, not only to more refined economic goods but to the highest goods of the mind and spirit. Add flying buttresses and spires to four walls and a roof, and a mere shelter for the body develops into a cathedral to house the spirit of man.

The Human Situation

There are three schools of thought as to man's economic nature and needs. First there are the economic determinists, who argue as if man were merely a soulless appendage to his material needs. For them, the modes of production at any given time decree the nature of man's institutions, his philosophies, and even his religions. Economics, under this dispensation, will be a tool of the state. On the opposite side of the fence is a school of thought which appears to regard it as a cosmic calamity that each soul is sullied by connection with a body which must be fed and kept warm. Spiritual purity will not be attained until there is deliverance from this incubus; but until that happy day, let us try to forget that man has creaturely needs which only the products of human labor can satisfy. Nothing in this scheme to dispose men to pay any attention to economics! But there is a third way.

The mainstream of the Judeo-Christian tradition is characterized by a robust earthiness which makes it as alien to the materialism of the first of the above alternatives as to the disembodied spirituality of the second. Soul and body are not at war with each other, but are parts of our total human nature. It is the whole man who needs to be saved, not just the soul. Creaturely needs are, therefore, legitimate, and being legitimate they sanction the economic activities by which alone they can be met.

Such an understanding of the human situation prepares us to accept the idea that economics is a discipline in its own right, governed by its own natural laws. This tradition also makes it plain that economic action is in the realm of means, and thus properly subject to noneconomic criteria. These noneconomic criteria are supplied by our religion, which deals with the meaning and purpose of this earthly life, and the destiny of man beyond it. When men have a lively sense of the spiritual dimension of their lives, they are in a good position to cope with the problems posed by the political and economic sectors; but when there is an erosion of spiritual values, the malaise there will be reflected at the social level as muddle in both the forum and market place.

There Is No Alternative to the Free Market Economy

I have been discussing the significance and some of the earmarks of economic life in a free society—a free society being one which limits its government by a written constitution to certain delegated functions. But are there not, some might ask, alternatives to the free market, private property economy? What about socialism, or the planned society? The answer to these questions is that there are many ways to liquidate an economy, but there is only one way to produce economic goods. There are no genuine alternatives to the free market economy. Every so-called alternative depends upon political redistribution. Political interventions in the economy deprive some people of what they produce for the assumed benefit of other people. This is to commit an injustice, and, of course, it diminishes production.

There is only one way for mankind to live and improve its economic circumstances, and that is by applying its energies to nature and nature's products. Goods are produced in this way and in no other. But once produced, the goods of some men may be acquired by other men through political manipulation. Every variety of socialism rests upon this practice. Let government perform this service and the trek to Washington is on. Once on, it will grow in geometric progression as group after group organizes to apply political pressure to get something for nothing; organized labor, the farm bloc, veterans, regional groups, educationists, the aged, and others.

Business and industry, strictly speaking, have to do only with the deploying of economic factors and resources—somebody making something, transporting it, exchanging it. A businessman or industrialist, pursuing his aims as an entrepreneur, seeks to turn a profit. The appearance of a profit indicates that his talents are being employed in a manner approved by a significant number of people. Absence of a profit, on the other hand, ought to be his clue that people are instructing him to go into some other line. So long as a man produces and sells things people want at prices they are willing to pay, he operates according to the rules of economics. The vast majority of our millions of business enterprises are conducted in this fashion. All that is necessary to keep this operation going is for the law to inhibit and penalize cases of theft, fraud, and violence.

Freedom Costs

Something like this was the dream of classical Liberalism. It was what Adam Smith had in mind when he spoke of "the liberal plan of equality, liberty, and justice."

Classical Liberalism meant freedom: freedom to write and speak, freedom to worship and teach, and, the most neglected freedom of all, freedom of economic enterprise, i.e., consumer sovereignty in the market place. A believer in free speech accepts this principle even though he is fully aware that its exercise will result in campaign oratory, socialist tracts, uplift drivel, pornography, public relations prose, modern poetry, and the "literature" of a beat generation. The defender of free speech recognizes these things as corruptions of the divine gift of communication, but they are part of the price he is willing to pay for freedom. Freedom costs, and thus it cannot endure among a people who do not understand this or, if they do, are unwilling to incur these costs.

Acceptance of the principle of economic liberty means that the consumer has a right to demand, and the producer a right to supply, any item which does not injure another—as injury is defined in laws against assault, theft, and fraud. This means that poor taste and doubtful morals will find expression here just as they do in the kindred fields of speech and religion. A rock-and-roll performer will ride around in a pink Cadillac while a symphony orchestra has to beg for funds. A race track will be built where common sense would dictate a playground. People refuse to buy mere transportation; they want a chariot with lots of chrome, tailfins, and three hundred horses under the hood.

Freedom costs, and the costs of freedom in the areas of speech, press, worship, and assemblage are generally acknowledged by a significant number of articulate people. These freedoms are not under assault—not in this country, at any rate. In the case of economic freedom, the situation is different. Few people mistake the abuses of free speech for the principle itself; but the abuses of economic liberty loom so large in the modern eye that it cannot detect the market principle of which they are violations.

And Government Must Be Limited

Freedom, in sound theory, is all of a piece. It hinges on properly limiting government. A society may be called free when its government does not dictate matters of religion and private conscience, does not censor reading material, curb speech, nor bar lawful assemblage. But mere paper guarantees of these important freedoms are worthless if there is governmental control and bureaucratic planning of economic life. The guarantee of religious freedom is worth little if the devotees are denied the economic means to build their temples, print their literature, and pay their spiritual guides. How meaningful is freedom of the press if there are no private means to buy paper and presses? And there is no full right to assemble if buildings, street corners, and vacant lots are government owned. "Whoso controls our subsistence controls us."

If government is properly limited, men are free. In a free society a certain pattern of economic activity will be precipitated. This pattern will change constantly. It will respond as men have less or more political liberty. It will be modified as technology advances, taste is refined, and morals improve. Properly speaking, the economic pattern of a free society is capitalism, or the market economy. Under capitalism the people are economically free, exercising control over their own subsistence, and thus they become self-controlling in other freedoms as well.

Part Three

Political Aspects

The tendency of governments to abuse powers delegated to them causes some victims to conclude that any government is evil. But anarchy is no part of the freedom philosophy. There is need for government to police the market and keep it open, to protect the life and the property of each peaceful person. The problem is to limit the powers of government to such defensive purposes.

This problem is here examined by an eminent French journalist and statesman of the nineteenth century, Frederic Bastiat; by author and former *Freeman* editor, Frank Chodorov, and by theologian, professor and college president, Perry Gresham.

5

Frederic Bastiat on Liberty
(selected excerpts)

The outcome of the eternal conflict between individual liberty and compulsory collectivism may well depend on the depth and quality of the study of those who devote their lives to it. Surrounding that academic nucleus are millions of concerned citizens, busy in other occupations, but hungering for reason and truth.

Once in a while comes a Frederic Bastiat (French economist, statesman, philosopher, 1801–1850), able to see the harmonious nature of the market and to see through the sophisms by socialists who would pervert the law into an instrument of plunder; able to present clearly and convincingly to concerned citizens the reason for and the truth about freedom.

What follows are samplings—a taste of his wisdom—an introduction to the books by Bastiat: Economic Harmonies, Economic Sophisms *and* Selected Essays on Political Economy.

Freedom and Harmony

The worst thing that can happen to a good cause is, not to be skillfully attacked, but to be ineptly defended.   *Sophisms, 107*

There is power only in principles: they alone are a beacon light for men's minds, a rallying point for convictions gone astray.

Essays, 113

Society is composed of men, and every man is a *free* agent. Since man is free, he can choose; since he can choose, he can err; since he can err, he can suffer. I go further: He must err and he must suffer; for his starting point is ignorance, and in his ignorance he sees before him an infinite number of unknown roads, all of which save one lead to error.   *Harmonies, xxx*

I do not call upon the state to compel everyone to accept my opinion, but, rather, not to force me to accept anybody else's opinion.   *Essays, 276*

If political economy attains to the insight that men's interests are harmonious, it does so because it does not stop, as socialism does, at the immediate consequences of phenomena, but goes on to their eventual and ultimate effects.   *Essays, 138*

Each advance over Nature, after first rewarding the initiative of a few men, soon becomes, by the operation of the law of competition, the gratuitous and common heritage of all mankind.
Harmonies, 416

The Market Economy

Self-interest is that indomitable individualistic force within us that urges us on to progress and discovery, but at the same time disposes us to monopolize our discoveries. Competition is that no less indomitable humanitarian force that wrests progress, as fast as it is made, from the hands of the individual and places it at the disposal of all mankind.   *Harmonies, 289*

By virtue of exchange, one man's prosperity is beneficial to all others.   *Harmonies, 82*

Capital has from the beginning of time worked to free men from the yoke of ignorance, want, and tyranny. To frighten away capital is to rivet a triple chain around the arms of the human race.
Harmonies, 190

Property, the right to enjoy the fruits of one's labor, the right to work, to develop, to exercise one's faculties, according to one's own understanding, without the state intervening otherwise than by its protective action—this is what is meant by liberty.
Essays, 109

Thanks to the nonintervention of the state in private affairs, wants and satisfactions would develop in their natural order. We should not see poor families seeking instruction in literature before they have bread. We should not see the city being populated at the expense of the country, or the country at the expense of the city. We should not see those great displacements of capital, of labor, and of population which are provoked by legislative measures, displacements that render the very sources of existence so uncertain and precarious, and thereby add so greatly to the responsibilities of the government.   *Essays, 53*

Law and Justice

Law is justice. And it is under the law of justice, under the rule of right, under the influence of liberty, security, stability, and responsibility, that every man will attain to the full worth and dignity of his being, and that mankind will achieve, in a calm and orderly way—slowly, no doubt, but surely—the progress to which it is destined.   *Essays, 94*

No society can exist if respect for the law does not to some extent prevail; but the surest way to have the laws respected is to make them respectable. When law and morality are in contradiction, the citizen finds himself in the cruel dilemma of either losing his moral sense or of losing respect for the law, two evils of which one is as great as the other, and between which it is difficult to choose.   *Essays, 56*

It is not because men have passed laws that personality, liberty, and property exist. On the contrary, it is because personality, liberty, and property already exist that men make laws.

Essays, 51

Law is the organization of the natural right to legitimate self-defense; it is the substitution of collective force for individual forces, to act in the sphere in which they have the right to act, to do what they have the right to do: to guarantee security of person, liberty, and property rights, to cause *justice* to reign over all.

Essays, 52

Government acts only by the intervention of force; hence, its action is legitimate only where the intervention of force is itself legitimate.   *Harmonies, 456*

A man who would consider himself a bandit if, pistol in hand, he prevented me from carrying out a transaction that was in conformity with my interests has no scruples in working and voting for a law that replaces his private force with the public force and subjects me, at my own expense, to the same unjust restriction. *Harmonies*, 463

State Intervention

The state tends to expand in proportion to its means of existence and to live beyond its means, and these are, in the last analysis, nothing but the substance of the people. Woe to the people that cannot limit the sphere of action of the state! Freedom, private enterprise, wealth, happiness, independence, personal dignity, all vanish. *Sophisms*, 141

What must be the consequence of all this intervention? . . . Capital, under the impact of such a doctrine, will hide, flee, be destroyed. And what will become, then, of the workers, those workers for whom you profess an affection so deep and sincere, but so unenlightened? Will they be better fed when agricultural production is stopped? Will they be better dressed when no one dares to build a factory? Will they have more employment when capital will have disappeared? *Essays*, 109

Where, at such a time, is the bold speculator who would dare set up a factory or engage in an enterprise? . . . What man in the whole country has the least knowledge of the position in which the law will forcibly place him and his line of work tomorrow? And, under such conditions, who can or will undertake anything? *Essays*, 107

The state is the great fictitious entity by which everyone seeks to live at the expense of everyone else. *Essays*, 144

Legal Plunder

No greater change nor any greater evil could be introduced into society than this: to convert the law into an instrument of plunder. *Essays*, 55

Illegal plunder fills everyone with aversion; it turns against itself all the forces of public opinion and puts them on the side of justice. Legal plunder, on the contrary, is perpetrated without troubling the conscience, and this cannot fail to weaken the moral fiber of a nation. *Essays*, 134

See whether the law takes from some what belongs to them in order to give it to others to whom it does not belong. We must see whether the law performs, for the profit of one citizen and to the detriment of others, an act which that citizen could not perform himself without being guilty of a crime. Repeal such a law without delay. It is not only an iniquity in itself; it is a fertile source of iniquities, because it invites reprisals, and if you do not take care, what begins by being an exception tends to become general, to multiply itself, and to develop into a veritable system.

Essays, 61

Legal plunder can be committed in an infinite number of ways; hence, there are an infinite number of plans for organizing it: tariffs, protection, bonuses, subsidies, incentives, the progressive income tax, free education, the right to employment, the right to profit, the right to wages, the right to relief, the right to the tools of production, interest free credit, etc., etc. And it is the aggregate of all these plans, in respect to what they have in common, legal plunder, that goes under the name of *socialism.*   *Essays,* 61

Plunderers conform to the Malthusian law: they multiply with the means of existence; and the means of existence of knaves is the credulity of their dupes. Seek as one will, there is no substitute for an informed and enlightened public opinion. It is the only remedy.

Sophisms, 139

6

The Source of Rights

by Frank Chodorov

The late Frank Chodorov edited The Freeman *for a time, was associate editor of* Human Events, *and the author of several books, including* The Income Tax *(New York: Devin Adair, 1954) from which this selection is reprinted by permission.*

This essay shows why a socialistic society must decline because it fails to respect private property.

The basic axiom of socialism, in all its forms, is that might is right. And that means that power is all there is to morality. If I am bigger and stronger than you and you have no way of defending yourself, then it is right if I thrash you; the fact that I did thrash you is proof that I had the right to do so. On the other hand, if you can intimidate me with a gun, then right returns to your side. All of which comes to mere nonsense. And a social order based on the socialistic axiom—which makes the government the final judge of all morality—is a nonsensical society. It is a society in which the highest value is the acquisition of power—as exemplified in a Hitler or a Stalin—and the fate of those who cannot acquire it is subservience as a condition of existence.

The senselessness of the socialistic axiom is shown by the fact that there would be no society, and therefore no government, if there were no individuals. The human being is the unit of all social institutions; without a man there cannot be a crowd. Hence, we are compelled to look to the individual to find an axiom on which to build a nonsocialistic moral code. What does he tell us about himself?

Desire to Live

In the first place, he tells us that above all things he wants to live. He tells us this even when he first comes into the world and lets out a yell. Because of that primordial desire, he maintains, he has a right to live. Certainly, nobody else can establish a valid claim to his life, and for that reason he traces his own title to an authority that transcends all men, to God. That title makes sense.

When the individual says he has a valid title to life, he means that all that is he, is his own: his body, his mind, his faculties. Maybe there is something else in life, such as a soul, but without going into that realm, he is willing to settle on what he knows about himself—his consciousness. All that is "I" is "mine." That implies, of course, that all that is "you" is "yours"—for, every "you" is an "I." Rights work both ways.

But, while just wanting to live gives the individual a title to life, it is an empty title unless he can acquire the things that make life liveable, beginning with food, raiment, and shelter. These things do not come to you because you want them; they come as the result of putting labor to raw materials. You have to give something of yourself—your brawn or your brain—to make the necessary things available. Even wild berries have to be picked before they can be eaten. But the energy you put out to make the necessary things is part of you; it *is* you. *Therefore, when you cause these things to exist, your title to yourself, your labor, is extended to the things. You have a right to them simply because you have a right to life.*

Source of Government

That is the moral basis of the right of property. "I own it because I made it" is a title that proves itself. The recognition of that title is implied in the statement that "I *make* so many dollars a week." That is literally true.

But what do you mean when you say you own the thing you produced? Say it is a bushel of wheat. You produced it to satisfy your desire for bread. You can grind the wheat into flour, bake the loaf of bread, eat it, or share it with your family or a friend. Or you can give part of the wheat to the miller in payment for his labor; the part you give him, in the form of wages, is his because he gave you labor in exchange. Or you sell half the bushel of wheat for money, which you exchange for butter to go with the bread. Or you put the money in the bank so that you can have something else later on, when you want it.

In other words, your ownership entitles you to use your judgment as to what you will do with the product of your labor—consume it, give it away, sell it, save it. Freedom of disposition is the substance of property rights.

Freedom of Disposition

Interference with this freedom of disposition is, in the final analysis, interference with your right to life. At least, that is your reaction to such interference, for you describe such interference with a word that expresses a deep emotion: You call it "robbery." What's more, if you find that this robbery persists, if you are regularly deprived of the fruits of your labor, you lose interest in laboring. The only reason you work is to satisfy your desires; and if experience shows that despite your efforts your desires go unsatisfied, you become stingy about laboring. You become a "poor" producer.

Suppose the freedom of disposition is taken away from you entirely. That is, you become a slave; you have no right of property. Whatever you produce is taken by somebody else; and though a good part of it is returned to you, in the way of sustenance, medical care, housing, you cannot under the law dispose of your output; if you try to, you become the legal "robber." Your concern in production wanes and you develop an attitude toward laboring that is called a "slave" psychology. Your interest in yourself also drops because you sense that without the right of property you are not much different from the other living things in the barn. The clergyman may tell you you are a man, with a soul; but you sense that without the right of property you are somewhat less of a man than the one who can dispose of your production as he wills. If you are a human, how human are you?

It is silly, then, to prate of human rights being superior to property rights, because the right of ownership is traceable to the right to life, which is certainly inherent in the human being. Property rights are in fact human rights.

A society built around the denial of this fact is, or must become, a slave society—although the socialists describe it differently. It is a society in which some produce and others dispose of their output. The laborer is not stimulated by the prospect of satisfying his desires but by fear of punishment. When his ownership is not interfered with, when he works for himself, he is inclined to develop his faculties of production because he has unlimited desires. He works for food, as a matter of necessity; but when he has a sufficiency of food, he begins to think of fancy dishes, a tablecloth, and music with his meals. There is no end of desires the human being can conjure up, and will work for, provided he feels reasonably sure that his labor will not be in vain. Contrariwise, when the law deprives him of the incentive of enjoyment, he will work only as necessity compels him. What use is there in putting out more effort?

Therefore, the general production of a socialistic society must decline to the point of mere subsistence.

Decline of Society

The economic decline of a society without property rights is followed by the loss of other values. It is only when we have a sufficiency of necessaries that we give thought to nonmaterial things, to what is called culture. On the other hand, we find we can do without books, or even moving pictures, when existence is at stake. Even more than that, we who have no right to own certainly have no right to give, and charity becomes an empty word; in a socialistic order, no one need give thought to an unfortunate neighbor because it is the duty of the government, the only property owner, to take care of him; it might even become a crime to give a "bum" a dime. When the denial of the right of the individual is negated through the denial of ownership, the sense of personal pride, which distinguishes man from beast, must decay from disuse . . .

Whatever else socialism is, or is claimed to be, its first tenet is the denial of private property. All brands of socialism, and there are many, are agreed that property rights must be vested in the political establishment. None of the schemes identified with this ideology, such as the nationalization of industry, or socialized medicine, or the abolition of free choice, or the planned economy, can become operative if the individual's claim to his property is recognized by the government.

7

Think Twice Before You Disparage Capitalism

by Perry E. Gresham

Dr. Gresham is a minister, educator, author, and President Emeritus, Bethany College in West Virginia. He was long a trustee of FEE. This article appeared in the March 1977 issue of The Freeman *and has been widely reprinted and distributed as a defense of competitive enterprise under limited government.*

"Everybody for himself, said the elephant as he danced around among the chickens." This lampoon of capitalism came from a Canadian politician. The word "capitalism" has fallen into disrepute. It is associated with other pejorative terms such as "fat cat," "big business," "military-industrial complex," "greedy industrialists," "stand patters," "reactionaries," and "property values without regard to human values." Many serious scholars look on capitalism as a transitional system between late feudalism and inevitable socialism.

Adam Smith has been associated with the word "capitalism" even though he did not use the term. He did not so much as refer to capital by that name, but used the word "stock" to describe what we call capital. Karl Marx wrote in response to Adam Smith's *Wealth of Nations* and called his great work *Das Kapital.* There was disparagement and scorn—even hate—for the ideas of the free market economy. The term capitalism has been less than appealing to many people since that time even though they know little about the contents of the Marx benchmark in political economy.

Some political economists who cherish individual liberty and the free market have suggested that a new name be found to describe economic liberty and individual responsibility. Until a new name appears, however, the thoughtful person does well to think twice before he disparages the market economy with all of its implications implied by the term capitalism since there is now no ready alternative available for reasonable discourse.

Is the System Outmoded?

Many thoughtful citizens of America think of capitalism as a quaint and vanishing vestige of our Yankee industrial beginnings. With burgeoning population, urbanization, and industrialization, they argue, capitalism disappears. They are not quite ready to embrace socialism, but they heartily approve government planning and intervention. John Kenneth Galbraith, articulate spokesman for the liberal establishment, calls for the open acclaim of a new socialism which he believes to be both imminent and necessary. "The new socialism allows of no acceptable alternatives; it cannot be escaped except at the price of grave discomfort, considerable social disorder and, on occasion, lethal damage to health and well-being. The new socialism is not ideological; it is compelled by circumstance." (*Economics and the Public Purpose,* 1973)

At first blush, the Marxian assumption of economic determinism is quite plausible, but I do not believe it can stand up to the scrutiny of experience. My study of history leads me to assume with many of my thoughtful colleagues that free people can, within certain limits, choose their own systems of political economy. This is precisely what happened in West Germany at the time of Ludwig Erhard. The Germans chose capitalism rather than the socialism recommended by many American, British, and Continental economists and politicians. It is my opinion that Americans can and should call for a renewal of capitalism rather than a new socialism.

Capitalism has been neither understood nor sympathetically considered by most contemporary Americans. Capitalism is a radical and appealing system of political economy which needs a new and favorable review. The new socialism has never been tried. The old socialism is not very inviting. Consider Russia, China,

Cuba, Chile, and now Britain. Capitalism has been tried with the most amazing success in all history. What is the nature of a political and economic system which has made the poor people of America more prosperous than the rich of many countries operating under State control? Here are my paragraphs in praise of capitalism. They are somewhat lyrical but grounded in fact and open to review.

An Enviable Record

Capitalism is the one system of political economy which works, has worked and, given a chance, will continue to work. The alternative system is socialism. Socialism is seductive in theory, but tends toward tyranny and serfdom in practice.

Capitalism was not born with *The Wealth of Nations,* nor will it die with *Das Kapital.* It is as old as history and as new as a paper route for a small boy. Capitalism is a point of view and a way of life. Its principles apply whether or not they are understood, approved, and cherished.

Capitalism is no relic of Colonial America. It has the genius of freedom to change with the times and to meet the challenges of big industries, big unions, and big government if it can free itself from the restraints of interest-group intervention which eventuates in needless government expansion and spending. Let the market work, and the ambition of each individual will serve the common good of society.

Capitalism is an economic system which believes with Locke and Jefferson that life, liberty, and property are among the inalienable rights of man.

Capitalism denies the banal dichotomy between property values and human values. Property values *are* human values. Imagine the disjunction when it is applied to a person with a mechanical limb or a cardiac pacemaker. The workman with his tools and the farmer with his land are almost as dramatic in the exemplification of the identity between a person and his property.

Capitalism is belief in man—an assumption that prosperity and happiness are best achieved when each person lives by his own will and his own intelligence. Each person is a responsible citizen.

Limited Government

Capitalism recognizes the potential tyranny of any government. The government is made for man, not man for the government. Therefore, government should be limited in size and function, lest free individuals lose their identity, become wards of the State. Frederic Bastiat has called the State a "great fiction wherein everybody tries to live at the expense of everybody else."

Capitalism denies the naive and mystic faith in the State to control wages and prices. A fair price is the amount agreed upon by the buyer and seller. Competition in a free market is far more trustworthy than any government administrator. The government is a worthy defense against force and fraud, but the market is much better at protecting against monopoly, inflation, soaring prices, depressed wages, and the problems of scarcity. Capitalism works to the advantage of consumer and worker alike.

Capitalism denies the right of government to take the property of a private citizen at will, or to tax away his livelihood at will, or to tell him when and where he must work or how and where he must live. Capitalism is built on the firm foundation of individual liberty.

Capitalism believes that every person deserves an opportunity. "All men are created equal" in terms of opportunity, but people are not equal—nor should they be. How dull a world in which nobody could outrun anybody! Competition is a good thing no matter how much people try to avoid it. Equality and liberty are contradictory. Capitalism chooses liberty!

Equality of Opportunity

Capitalism gives a poor person an opportunity to become rich. It does not lock people into the condition of poverty. It calls on every individual to help his neighbor, but not to pauperize him by making him dependent. Independence for every person is the capitalist ideal.

When a person contracts to work for a day, a week, or a month before he is paid, he is practicing capitalism. It is a series of contracts for transactions to be completed in the future. Capitalism is promise and fulfillment.

Capitalism offers full employment to those who wish to work. The worker is free to accept a job at any wage he can get. He can join with his fellows in voluntary association to improve his salary and working conditions. He can change jobs or start his own business. He relies on his ability to perform rather than on the coercive power of the State to force his employment.

Capitalism is color-blind. Black, brown, yellow, red, and white are alike in the market place. A person is regarded for his ability rather than his race. Economic rewards in the market place, like honor and acclaim on the playing field, are proportionate to performance. The person who has the most skill, ability, and ingenuity to produce is paid accordingly by the people who value and need his goods and services.

Trust in the Market

Capitalism is a belief that nobody is wise enough and knows enough to control the lives of other people. When each person buys, sells, consumes, produces, saves, and spends at will, what Leonard Read calls "the miracle of the market" enables everyone to benefit.

Capitalism respects the market as the only effective and fair means of allocating scarce goods. A free market responds to shortages and spurs production by raising prices. Arbitrary controls merely accept and keep the shortages. When rising prices inspire human ingenuity to invent and produce, the goods return and prices fall.

Nobody knows enough to build an airplane or a computer, but hundreds of people working together perform these amazing acts of creation. This is the notable human achievement which Adam Smith called "The Division of Labor."

Capitalism derives its name from the fact that capital is essential to the success of any venture whether it involves an individual, a corporation, or a nation-state. Capital is formed by thrift. The person who accumulates capital is personally rewarded and, at the same time, a public benefactor.

Capitalism makes every person a trustee of what he has. It appoints him general manager of his own life and property, and it holds him responsible for that trusteeship.

Church and Family Ties

Capitalism is a natural ally of religion. The Judeo-Christian doctrines of stewardship and vocation are reflected in a free market economy. Churches and synagogues can be free and thriving with capitalism. When the churches falter, the moral strength of capitalism is diminished.

Capitalism depends on the family for much of its social and moral strength. When the family disintegrates, the capitalist order falls into confusion and disarray. The motive power for the pursuit of life, liberty, and property is in the filial and parental love of a home with its dimensions of ancestry and posterity.

Capitalism enables entrepreneurs to be free people, taking their own risks and collecting their own rewards.

Work is a privilege and a virtue under capitalism. Leisure is honored, but idleness is suspect. The idea that work is a scourge and a curse has no place in the climate of capitalism.

Capitalism holds profits derived from risk and investment to be as honorable as wages or rent. Dividends paid to those who invest capital in an enterprise are as worthy as interest paid to a depositor in a savings bank. The idea abroad that risk capital is unproductive is patently false.

The Voluntary Way

Capitalism honors and promotes charity and virtue. True charity cannot be compelled. Universities, hospitals, social agencies, are more satisfactory and more fun when they derive from voluntary support. Money taken by force and bestowed by formula is no gift.

The consumer is sovereign under capitalism. No bureaucrat, marketing expert, advertiser, politician, or self-appointed protector can tell him what to buy, sell, or make.

Capitalism encourages invention, innovation, and technological advance. Creativity cannot be legislated. Only free people can bring significant discovery to society. Thomas A. Edison was not commissioned by the government.

The concept of free and private enterprise applies to learning and living as well as to the production of goods and services. When a student learns anything it is his own. Nobody, let alone a state, ever taught anybody anything. The State can compel conformity of a sort, but genuine learning is an individual matter—an act of free enterprise and discovery.

Respect for the Individual

Capitalism honors the liberty and dignity of every person. The private citizen is not regarded as a stupid dupe to every crook and con man. He is regarded as a free citizen under God and under the law—able to make his own choices, not a ward of the State who must be protected by his self-appointed superiors who administer government offices.

Capitalism is a system which distributes power to the worker, the young, the consumer, and the disadvantaged by offering freedom for voluntary organization, dissent, change, choice, and political preference, without hindrance from the police power of government.

The renewal of capitalism could be the renewal of America. Nothing could be more radical, more timely, or more beneficial to the responsible and trustworthy common people who are now beguiled by the soft and seductive promises of the new socialism.

No political and economic system is perfect. Plato's *Republic* was in heaven—not on earth. If people were all generous and good, any system would work. Since people are self-centered, they are more free and happy in a system which allows the avarice and aggressiveness of each to serve the best interest of all. Capitalism is such a system. It is modestly effective even in chains. The time has come for daring people to release it and let us once more startle the world with the initiative and productivity of free people!

Some of my academic colleagues will deny, dispute, or scorn the foregoing laudatory comments about capitalism. They will say that socialism benefits the poor, the young, the consumer, the minorities, and that capitalism protects the rich and the powerful. When discussion is joined, however, they will argue in terms of politics rather than economics, ideology rather than empirical evidence, and they will accuse me of doing the same. When the most persuasive case is produced, it will not convince. Political opinions are not changed by rational argument.

A Call for Renewal

Those who have socialist ideological preferences are merely annoyed to the point of arrogance and disdain by such honest appreciation of capitalism as I have presented. Those scholars, however, who like Ludwig von Mises, Friedrich Hayek, and Milton Friedman have explored the relevance of capitalism to our present predicament, will join in the call for renewal of a system that works. Those who, like the late Joseph Schumpeter, have watched the apparently relentless disintegration of capitalism, and have concluded that socialism will work, albeit with painful disadvantages, will heave a long sad sigh of regret at the passing of the happy and prosperous capitalist way of life. They will, as people must, accept what appears from their perspective inevitable, and try to make the best of the gray and level life of socialism.

Schumpeter, however, was no defeatist. He was a perceptive analyst of human affairs. In the preface to the second edition of his *magnum opus* he wrote, "This, finally, leads to the charge of 'defeatism.' I deny entirely that this term is applicable to a piece of analysis. Defeatism denotes a certain psychic state that has meaning only in reference to action. Facts in themselves and inferences from them can never be defeatist or the opposite whatever that might be. The report that a given ship is sinking is not defeatist. Only the spirit in which this report is received can be defeatist: The crew can sit down and drink. But it can also rush to the pumps." (*Capitalism, Socialism and Democracy*, 1950).

Friends of liberty, to the pumps!

Those who love liberty more than equality, those who are uneasy with unlimited government, those who have faith in man's ability to shape his own destiny, those who have marveled at the miracle of the market will join me in this call for renewal of this simple, reasonable, versatile, and open system of capitalism which has worked, is working, and will work if freed from the fetters of limitless state intervention. The choice, I believe, is ours. The alternative is the stifling sovereign State.

Part Four

Moral Foundation

Important as are the economic and political aspects of the freedom philosophy, they cannot stand alone or together without a firm moral foundation. Freedom is a matter of personal choice, a moral choice, a chance to do as one ought.

The alternative is some form of compulsory collectivism, which denies the dignity of the individual and the freedom to choose.

The morality of freedom is examined here by Ralph Husted, a businessman from Indiana, and by the late Dr. F. A. Harper, teacher, former staff member of FEE, and later founder and president of the Institute for Humane Studies.

8

The Moral Foundation of Freedom

by Ralph Husted

Every year—indeed every day—is an appropriate time to review the moral foundation of our Republic. Such a review appeared in the March 1966 Freeman, *prepared by Ralph W. Husted, an Indiana businessman and long a close friend of the Foundation for Economic Education. Here now, slightly condensed, is his testimony for your enjoyment and guidance.*

I never miss an opportunity, when I am in Philadelphia, to look at that small room where the architects of this nation in a relatively short time drafted, debated, and finally adopted the Constitution. The vision of a great republic was given to a handful of men who, when opportunity came, were prepared by education, courage, and faith to discharge one of the greatest responsibilities ever undertaken by men.

I do not believe it was an accident that those men were brought together at the same time and at the same place in history. I think it was no accident that among that small group were some of the greatest thinkers of their day.

To one who sees about him a world of infinite plan and design, things do not just happen. There were times, we are told, when the Constitutional Convention approached disruption. I believe the fact that it was finally successful was not an accident. I believe the courage and wisdom demonstrated on that occasion were not accidental. And I believe it was no accident that Madison was able to draft in a short time a document containing the wisdom of ages, and at which men have marveled ever since.

The man who sees history as a great laboratory in which it has been proved time and again that cause has its inevitable effect, according to the design of a power greater than any of us can envision, cannot believe that the birth, education, and experience of Washington, Adams, Hamilton, Jefferson, and Madison were mere accidents of history and that the founding of America was merely a fortunate coincidence of men and circumstances.

Our Founding Fathers believed that we live in an ordered universe. They believed themselves to be a part of the universal order of things. Stated another way—they believed in God. They believed that every man must find his own place in a world where a place has been made for him. They sought independence for their nation but, more importantly, they sought freedom for individuals; freedom for men as individuals to think and act for themselves.

There, in Philadelphia, they established a republic dedicated to one purpose above all others—the preservation of individual liberty, the protection of a society where men would be free to pursue their purposes in life as they see them. They did not think man's purpose in life is to be determined by government or that government has any business deciding what purposes our society shall serve.

Spiritual, Economic, Political

When we speak of individual liberty, just what do we mean? In final analysis, I think it has three essential elements—namely: freedom of worship, economic freedom, and political freedom.

Freedom of worship meant to our forefathers exactly what the words imply, i.e., freedom to worship as one pleases. But remember, it also meant to them the right not to worship at all. We know, of course, that very few of them were disposed to make that choice. For most of them, worshiping God was an essential part of their lives. It is true that they believed in and advocated the separation of church and state, but they certainly did not believe in separation of the people from God.

There is an additional point I want to make in connection with religious freedom, and it leads to the central idea of what I have to say here. *Religious freedom means nothing without economic and political freedom.* Life is not divided into neat little compartments one of which can be considered without regard to all others. Life can't be divided, nor can freedom. It is impossible to have religious freedom without political and economic freedom. It is equally impossible to have economic or political freedom without religious freedom. Now let us consider economic freedom in that light.

Importance of Economic Freedom

Economic freedom means, literally, freedom to seek the means of satisfying one's material needs; but I doubt that any man ever considered his own well-being in terms of material needs alone. Consideration of man's material needs necessarily involves thinking at the same time about his spiritual needs, because his well-being depends upon satisfaction of both, and both consciously or unconsciously influence his efforts to satisfy his wants. Hence the interdependence of economic and religious freedom.

The significance of economic freedom lies in the very nature of creation. We are made one at a time, and no two of us alike. The differences between us are great, and by far the greatest differences are spiritual. The bare necessities of life are few but the number of material things necessary to give expression to the spirit of mankind is endless.

The millions of forms in which property is molded by the hand of man and the millions of uses to which it is put are but extensions of the millions of human personalities who gather property and adapt it to their needs. Whether it be a pencil or a steel mill, property is but a reflection of the infinite spirit of man. It reflects the desire of the human spirit for self-expression.

If you agree with this, I think you will also agree that property, to serve its purpose best, must be private property. By the very nature of creation, no two of us can have the same desires, the same skills, or the same mental endowments. No two of us can express ourselves in the same way. Property cannot possibly serve the same purpose for one owner as it serves for others. What we call ownership is the right to the use, possession, control, and disposition of property; and it is these incidents of ownership which make property useful in satisfying the needs of individuals.

Clearly, therefore, ownership must be private if a particular item of property is to satisfy the needs of a particular man as he and no one else sees them. If you still have doubt as to the necessity for private ownership of property, consider for a moment that all of us are property owners; a man's labor is his property, and unless he is free to control and dispose of his labor as he wishes, he is a slave.

Men have coordinated their efforts in countless ways to satisfy their material wants, but always, and regardless of how interdependent their lives may become, their efforts are directed to satisfaction of the wants of individuals. Men have created business organizations both large and small, both simple and complex, but such organizations have no life, no philosophy, and no ability to create or produce separate and apart from the individuals comprising them.

An organization or corporation may become so large that a person begins to feel his individuality is completely swallowed up in it, but the fact remains that he is the one endowed with life and not the organization. Only individuals can grow and progress, and only individuals can generate economic progress. Only an individual can want. Only an individual can know what he wants; and unless he is free to make the choices that will satisfy his wants, he is not really free.

Complex as our system may be, it is, nevertheless, built upon something that all of us understand—the promise of one man to another. It is built on the right to contract, to contract freely without the intervention of government. It is built on freedom of individual choice. A planned society may enforce specialization of work, but compulsion has never performed the miracles of production that have become commonplace among men who are able to contract as they wish.

Meaning of Political Freedom

Now, what about political freedom? Political freedom in the minds of many people is something which they define vaguely by the word "democracy," and which they associate with freedom of speech and the right to vote. To think of political freedom only as democracy is dangerous indeed because a democracy can become a tyrannical mob. To think of political freedom only as freedom of speech and the right to vote is to fall into a socialist trap, because even the socialists profess to believe in both. The right to vote may be essential to freedom, but we should remember that time and again people have given away their freedom by majority vote.

Then what do we mean by political freedom? I think it is this. Every right which we insist upon as free men carries with it the duty not to interfere forcibly with the enjoyment of the same right by others. Man's desire for self-expression is natural and good and the right to self-expression is essential, but unless it is accompanied by a proper sense of responsibility it may manifest itself in the use of force.

We are responsible beings but we all know that in the present state of civilization, and as it probably will be for ages to come, no one is or will be perfect. No one has or will have a perfect sense of right and wrong. We must, therefore, have the rule of law to restrain the use of force.

But let us also keep this in mind. The law is not self-executing. The law itself must employ force or the threat of force to restrain those who would act irresponsibly. It may seem trite to repeat here that "that government governs best which governs least," but it needs to be said now as much as when first spoken.

Political freedom means freedom from government restraint or compulsion beyond what is needed to curb irresponsible men. When government goes further than that, it becomes the oppressor of freedom. When we turn over to government the job of planning, managing, or controlling any undertaking, regardless of how humanitarian it may appear to be, we must weigh the cost in loss of freedom because loss of freedom inevitably accompanies the delegation of such power.

The Role of Government

Now, some of you may ask, "What about the many services which the government renders for the people? Does not the government do for us many things which we could not do for ourselves?" Does it? Perhaps we have been deluding ourselves. Dr. F. A. Harper has said:

> The government . . . cannot possibly do anything that people can't do for themselves, for the simple reason that people comprise all that is government. Government is manned by the very same persons whose deficiencies are presumed to disappear when com-

bined into a legal structure with bureaucratic, political trappings—
a process which makes an ordinary person, if anything, less able
than before to accomplish things.

Edmund Burke once said:

> To make a government requires no great prudence. Settle the seat
> of power; teach obedience; and the work is done. To give freedom
> is still more easy. It is not necessary to guide; it only requires to let
> go the rein. But to form a free government, that is, to temper
> together these opposite elements of liberty and restraint in one
> consistent work, requires much thought, deep reflection, a saga-
> cious, powerful, and combining mind.

It was no accident that George Washington and his contempo-
raries established something the world had never before seen, a
nation dedicated to freedom of the individual. Theirs were the
minds which understood that the only real liberty is individual
liberty. Theirs were the powerful and combining minds which
understood the moral foundation of freedom—man's personal
relationship with his Creator—and they made that the foundation
for the greatest nation on earth.

The Danger We Face

Today we are faced with the most serious attack on our freedom
which has ever confronted us. I say the most serious because it is
an attack on the very moral foundation which I have just
described. It is little comfort to know that the attack may have
been inspired initially by people beyond our borders. The disturb-
ing fact is that the burden of the attack is now being carried by
persons in all walks of life who profess to be and think they are
good Americans.

I think it has not been a case of knowingly abandoning our faith,
but rather we have been led without thinking to accept many
beliefs which in fact deny that men have a personal relationship
with God. Individual liberty has been sacrificed and government
has come to be looked upon, primarily, as an instrument for social
and economic planning.

We have allowed to infect our political philosophy the belief that men are no longer able to take care of themselves. We have established an enormous bureaucracy to plan for them. We still profess the need for religious freedom, but we have repudiated the conviction of our forefathers—that unless we also have economic and political freedom, religious freedom is meaningless.

We have, for example, adopted a graduated income tax for the avowed purpose of supporting essential government functions, but we have changed our concept of what is essential and we are now using the tax in shocking measure for the redistribution of wealth and as a means of controlling the lives of people.

We have subsidies for housing, subsidies for farmers, subsidies for power, subsidies for shipping, and subsidies for the aged. We take one man's property to give to another and think it is right simply because it is accomplished by majority vote. We have adopted the Marxist principle of "from each according to ability, to each according to need."

We have outright government ownership of hundreds of enterprises. We have government interference with the right to contract in practically every area of economic activity. In many areas such interference is so great that the free market, freedom of economic choice, is gone. We have allowed ourselves to think that a little socialism will not hurt us, but the acorn has now grown into a giant of the forest.

The Mixed-Up Economy

Many of our politicians, political scientists, economists, school textbook writers, and even some of our financial and industrial leaders see great hope for the future in what they call a mixed system of private enterprise and public enterprise. They speak of the "public sector" of our economy as contrasted with the "private sector" and of the necessity for a partnership between the two. They praise what is now fashionably called the partnership of government and business. They speak of the marvelous adaptability of our system of free enterprise because, as they say, it has been able to join hands with government to meet what government planners consider the needs of society.

What kind of partnership is it where one partner is supported entirely by the other? What kind of partnership is it where one has become such a burden to the other that there is evidence of the load becoming too great? How long can it last?

We have accepted fiscal immorality as a national policy. This is not something that has been forced upon us. The fact is that we insist upon it. Every downturn in business is the occasion for further demands that the government increase spending, that the Federal Reserve system reduce interest rates and buy government bonds so as to increase the supply of bank credit. All this, of course, results in an increase in the supply of spendable dollars but contributes nothing to the real wealth of the people. People are really not better off, because dollars are not wealth, nor are dollars a true measure of wealth when they are subject to devaluation by arbitrarily increasing the supply of them.

If one concedes that private property is indispensable to the achievement of man's happiness, then it must also be conceded that any artificial manipulation of the medium of exchange by which the value of property is measured is morally wrong. Yet that is exactly what our federal government does when it tinkers with interest rates to expand or restrict credit, or reduces reserve requirements, or puts pressure on the Federal Reserve system to buy or sell government bonds to increase or decrease bank credit, or engages in deficit spending. Money that is subject to tinkering by government becomes the instrument by which people are robbed of their property.

By Majority Vote in the Name of Democracy

We have done it all by majority vote and in the name of democracy. Now I do not want to be misunderstood. The word democracy still has meaning to me and I believe in it, but I would ask you to remember always that democracy is not an end in itself. Despite the preaching of our present-day textbook writers and government social planners, democracy is not the goal of America. Democracy can be and has been many times an instrument for the abuse of individuals. Our goal is, and must continue to be, individual freedom.

Of course we believe that everyone should have a decent house, that a farmer should enjoy a high standard of living, and that the aged should not want. But how are these things to be accomplished—by resorting to more economic and social planning by government and to a program of massive government spending?

Shall we ignore the fact that when we speak of government planning we presuppose the existence in government of someone with superhuman wisdom to do the planning? Shall we ignore the fact that when government does the planning, the coercive powers of government will be used to carry the plans into effect at an enormous sacrifice of individual freedom? Apparently some of our present-day leaders, both in government and out, believe we should.

Shall we accept the notion that merely because government planning for the people is done under the label of democracy, and is claimed to represent the interests of a majority of the people, it is right?

Today many of our people, both in government and out, believe the "welfare of the majority" is the criterion by which we should measure the extent of government interference in and control of economic affairs. We find people, both in government and out, urging an expanded program of government planning and spending in order, as they say, to improve society and strengthen freedom. We find today wholehearted endorsement of the idea that men are entitled, as a matter of right, to favorable working conditions, just pay, social security, adequate housing, and an adequate standard of living.

Of course, these things are desirable, but let me remind you that in the America conceived by our Founding Fathers, man's inalienable rights—life, liberty, and the right to own property—are not granted by the state. They are God-given. A decent house, adequate pay, and social security are not God-given. God gives men the capacity to acquire these things for themselves, but no more.

God gives men the capacity and freedom to work and create. He gives them nothing they can create for themselves. We renounce the great religious heritage handed down to us by our Founding Fathers when we speak of the material things which men are intended to work for as though they too are something we have a God-given right to demand.

If we believe as our Founding Fathers did, then we must let man be free to develop his sense of responsibility in his own way, and we must have faith that he will. When we come to understand that all men are endowed with the divine spirit, I think then, and only then, will we understand why men were meant to be free.

9

Morals and Liberty

by F. A. Harper

Dr. Harper was Professor of Marketing at Cornell University before joining the staff of FEE in 1946. Later he founded and served as President of the Institute for Humane Studies. This article was published as a FEE pamphlet in 1951, setting forth the moral postulates of the freedom philosophy and the immorality of the welfare state.

To many persons, the Welfare State has become a symbol of morality and righteousness. This makes those who favor the Welfare State appear to be the true architects of a better world; those who oppose it, immoral rascals who might be expected to rob banks or to do almost anything in defiance of ethical conduct. But is this so? Is the banner of morality, when applied to the concept of the Welfare State, one that is true or false?

I should like to pose five fundamental ethical concepts as postulates, by which to test the morality or immorality of the Welfare State. They are the ethical precepts found in the true Christian religion—true to its original foundations—and they are likewise found in other religious faiths, wherever and under whatever name these other religious concepts assist persons to perceive and practice the moral truths of human conduct.

Moral Postulate No. 1

Economics and morals are both parts of one inseparable body of truth. They must, therefore, be in harmony with one another. What is right morally must also be right economically, and vice versa. Since morals are a guide to betterment and to self-protection, economic policies which conflict with moral conduct must with certainty cause degeneration and self-destruction.

This postulate may seem simple and self-evident. Yet many economists and others of my acquaintance, including one who was a most capable and admired teacher, draw some kind of an impassable line of distinction between morals and economics. Such persons fail to test their economic concepts against their moral precepts. Some even scorn the moral base for testing economic concepts, as though it would somehow pollute their economic purity.

A highly capable theological scholar once said that only a short time before, for the first time, he had come to realize the close connection and inter-harmony that exist between morals and economics. He had always reserved one compartment for his religious thought and another separate one for his economic thought. "Fortunately," he said, in essence, "my economic thinking happened to be in harmony with my religious beliefs but it frightens me now to realize the risk I was taking in ignoring the harmony that must exist between the two."

This viewpoint—that there is no necessary connection between morals and economics—is all too prevalent. It explains, I believe, why immoral economic acts are tolerated, if not actively promoted, by persons of high repute who otherwise may be considered to be persons of high moral standards.

Moral Postulate No. 2

There is a force in the universe which no mortal can alter. Neither you nor I nor any earthly potentate with all his laws and edicts can alter this universal force, no matter how great one's popularity in his position of power. Some call this force God. Others call it Natural Law. Still others call it the Supernatural. But no matter how one may wish to name it, there is a force which rules and never surrenders to any mortal man or group of men— a force that is oblivious to anyone who presumes to elevate himself and his wishes above its rule.

This concept of universal force is the basis for all relationships of cause and consequence. It is the foundation for all science, including things not yet resolved as well as past discoveries.

It encompasses the older sciences such as astronomy, physics, and chemistry; it encompasses, in like manner, all human affairs.

Scientific discovery means the unveiling to human perception of something that has always existed. If it had not existed prior to the discovery—even though we were ignorant of it—it could not have been there to be discovered. That is the meaning of the concept of Natural Law. The so-called Law of Gravity is one expression of it.

This view—that there exists a Natural Law which rules over the affairs of human conduct—will be challenged by some who point out that man possesses the capacity for choice, that man's activity reflects a quality lacking in the chemistry of a stone and in the physical principle of the lever. But this trait of man—this capacity for choice—does not release him from the rule of cause and effect, which he can neither veto nor alter. What the capacity for choice means, instead, is that he is thereby enabled, by his own choice, to act either wisely or unwisely—that is, in either accord or discord with the truths of Natural Law. But once he has made his choice, the inviolate rule of cause and consequence takes over with an iron hand of justice, and delivers unto the doer either a reward or a penalty, as the consequence of his choice.

It is important, at this point, to note that morality presumes the existence of choice. One cannot be truly moral except as there exists the option of being immoral, and except as he selects the moral rather than the immoral option. In the admirable words of Thomas Davidson: "That which is not free is not responsible, and that which is not responsible is not moral." This means that free choice is a prerequisite of morality.

If I surrender my freedom of choice to a ruler—by vote or otherwise—I am still subject to the superior rule of Natural Law. Although I am subservient to the ruler who orders me to violate Truth, I must still pay the penalty for the evil or foolish acts in which I engage at his command.

Under this postulate—that there is a force in the universe which no mortal can alter—ignorance is no excuse to those who violate it, because Natural Law rules over the consequences of wisdom. This is true whether the ignorance is accompanied by good intentions or not; whether it is carried out under the name of some religion or the Welfare State or whatnot.

What, then, is the content of a basic moral code? What are the rules which, if followed, will better the condition of men?

Moral Postulate No. 3

The Golden Rule and the Decalogue, and their near equivalents in other great religions, provide the basic moral codes for man's conduct. The Golden Rule and the Decalogue are basic moral guides having priority over all other considerations. It is these which have guided the conduct of man in all progressive civilizations. With their violation has come the downfall of individuals and civilizations.

Some may prefer as a moral code something like: "Do as God would have us do," or "Do as Jesus would have done." But such as these, alone, are not adequate guides to conduct unless they are explained further, or unless they serve as symbolic of a deeper specific meaning. What *would* God have us do? What *would* Jesus have done? Only by adding some guides such as the Golden Rule and the Ten Commandments can we know the answers to these questions.

The Golden Rule—the rule of refraining from imposing on others what I would not have them impose on me—means that moral conduct for one is moral conduct for another; that there is not one set of moral guides for Jones and another for Smith; that the concept of equality under Moral Law is a part of morality itself. This alone is held by many to be an adequate moral code. But in spite of its importance as part of the moral code of conduct in this respect, the Golden Rule is not, it seems to me, sufficient unto itself. It is no more sufficient than the mere admonition, "Do good," which leaves undefined what is good and what is evil. The murderer, who at the time of the crime felt justified in committing it, can quote the Golden Rule in self-defense: "If I had done what that so-and-so did, and had acted as he acted, I would consider it fair and proper for someone to murder me." And likewise the thief may argue that if he were like the one he has robbed, or if he were a bank harboring all those "ill-gotten gains," he would consider himself the proper object of robbery. Some claim that justification for the Welfare State, too, is to be found in the Golden Rule. So, in addition to the Golden Rule, further rules are needed as guides for moral conduct.

The Decalogue embodies the needed guides on which the Golden Rule can function. But within the Ten Commandments, the two with which we are especially concerned herein are "Thou shalt not steal" and "Thou shalt not covet."

The Decalogue serves as a guide to moral conduct which, if violated, brings upon the violator a commensurate penalty. There may be other guides to moral conduct which one might wish to add to the Golden Rule and the Decalogue, as supplements or substitutes. But they serve as the basis on which others are built. Their essence, in one form or another, seems to run through all great religions. That, I believe, is not a happenstance, because if we embrace them as a guide to our conduct, our conduct will be both morally and economically sound.

This third postulate embodies what are judged to be the *principles* which should guide individual conduct as infallibly as the compass should guide the mariner. "Being practical" is a common popular guide to conduct; principles are scorned, if not forgotten. Those who scorn principles assert that it is foolish to concern ourselves with them because it is hopeless to expect their complete adoption by everyone. But does this fact make a principle worthless? Are we to conclude that the moral code against murder is worthless because of its occasional violation? Or that the compass is worthless because not everyone pursues to the ultimate the direction which it indicates? Or that the Law of Gravity is made impractical or inoperative by someone walking off a cliff and meeting death because of his ignorance of this principle? No. A principle remains a principle in spite of its being ignored or violated—or even unknown. A principle, like a compass, gives one a better sense of direction, if he is wise enough to know and to follow its guidance.

Moral Postulate No. 4

Moral principles are not subject to compromise. The Golden Rule and the Decalogue, as representing moral principles, are precise and strict. They are not a code of convenience. A principle can be broken, but it cannot be bent.

If the Golden Rule and the Decalogue were to be accepted as a code of convenience, to be laid aside or modified whenever "necessity seems to justify it" (whenever, that is, one desires to act in violation of them), they would not then be serving as moral guides. A moral guide which is to be followed only when one would so conduct himself anyhow, in its absence, has no effect on his conduct, and is not a guide to him at all.

The unbending rule of a moral principle can be illustrated by some simple applications. According to one Commandment, it is wholly wrong to steal all your neighbor's cow; it is also wholly wrong to steal half your neighbor's cow, not half wrong to steal half your neighbor's cow. Robbing a bank is wrong in principle, whether the thief makes off with a million dollars or a hundred dollars or one cent. A person can rob a bank of half its money, but in the sense of moral principle there is no way to half rob a bank; you either rob it or you do not rob it.

In like manner, the Law of Gravity is precise and indivisible. One either acts in harmony with this law or he does not. There is no sense in saying that one has only half observed the Law of Gravity if he falls off a cliff only half as high as another cliff off which he might have fallen.

Moral laws are strict. They rule without flexibility. They know not the language of man; they are not conversant with him in the sense of compassion. They employ no man-made devices like the suspended sentence; "Guilty" or "Not guilty" is the verdict of judgment by a moral principle.

As moral guides, the Golden Rule and the Decalogue are not evil and dangerous things, like a pain-killing drug, to be taken in cautious moderation, if at all. Presuming them to be the basic guides of what is right and good for civilized man, one cannot overindulge in them. Good need not be practiced in moderation.

Moral Postulate No. 5

Good ends cannot be attained by evil means. As stated in the second postulate, there is a force controlling cause and consequence which no mortal can alter, in spite of any position of influence or power which he may hold. Cause and consequence are linked inseparably.

An evil begets an evil consequence; a good, a good consequence. Good intentions cannot alter this relationship. Nor can ignorance of the consequence change its form. Nor can words. For one to say, after committing an evil act, "I'm sorry, I made a mistake," changes not one iota the consequence of the act; repentance, at best, can serve only to prevent repetition of the evil act, and perhaps assure the repeter a more preferred place in a Hereafter. But repentance *alone* does not bring back to life a murdered person, nor return the loot to the one who was robbed. Nor does it, I believe, fully obliterate the scars of evil on the doer himself.

Nor does saying, "He told me to do it," change the consequence of an evil act into a good one. For an evildoer to assert, "But it was the law of my government, the decree of my ruler," fails to dethrone God or to frustrate the rule of Natural Law.

The belief that good ends are attainable through evil means is one of the most vicious concepts of the ages. The political blueprint, *The Prince,* written around the year 1500 by Machiavelli, outlined this notorious doctrine. And for the past century it has been part and parcel of the kit of tools used by the Marxian communist-socialists to mislead people. Its use probably is as old as the conflict between temptation and conscience, because it affords a seemingly rational and pleasant detour around the inconveniences of one's conscience.

We know how power-hungry persons have gained political control over others by claiming that they somehow possess a special dispensation from God to do good through the exercise of means which our moral code identifies as evil. Thus arises a multiple standard of morals. It is the device by which immoral persons attempt to discredit the Golden Rule and the Decalogue, and make them inoperative.

Yet if one will stop to ponder the question just a little, he must surely see the unimpeachable logic of this postulate: Good ends cannot be attained by evil means. This is because the end pre-exists in the means, just as in the biological field we know that the seed of continued likeness pre-exists in the parent. Likewise in the moral realm, there is a similar moral reproduction wherein like begets like. This precludes the possibility of evil means leading to good ends. Good begets good; evil, evil. Immoral means cannot beget a good end, any more than snakes can beget roses.

The concept of the Welfare State can now be tested against the background of these five postulates: (1) Harmony exists between moral principles and wise economic practices. (2) There is a Universal Law of Cause and Effect, even in the areas of morals and economics. (3) A basic moral code exists in the form of the Golden Rule and the Decalogue. (4) These moral guides are of an uncompromising nature. (5) Good ends are attainable only through good means.

Moral Right to Private Property

Not all the Decalogue, as has been said, is directly relevant to the issue of the Welfare State. Its program is an economic one, and the only parts of the moral code which are directly and specifically relevant are these: (1) Thou shalt not steal. (2) Thou shalt not covet.

Steal what? Covet what? Private property, of course. What else could I steal from you, or covet of what is yours? I cannot steal from you or covet what you do not own as private property. Thus we find that the individual's right to private property is an unstated assumption which underlies the Decalogue. Otherwise these two admonitions would be empty of either purpose or meaning.

The right to have and to hold private property is not to be confused with the recovery of stolen property. If someone steals your car, it is still—by this moral right—your car rather than his; and for you to repossess it is merely to bring its presence back into harmony with its ownership. The same reasoning applies to the recovery of equivalent value if the stolen item itself is no longer returnable; and it applies to the recompense for damage done to one's own property by trespass or other willful destruction of private property. These means of protecting the possession of private property, and its use, are part of the mechanisms used to protect the moral right to private property.

Another point of possible confusion has to do with coveting the private property of another. There is nothing morally wrong in the admiration of something that is the property of another. Such admiration may be a stimulus to work for the means with which to buy it, or one like it. The moral consideration embodied in this Commandment has to do with thoughts and acts leading to the violation of the other Commandment, though still short of actual theft.

The moral right to private property, therefore, is consistent with the moral codes of all the great religious beliefs. It is likely that a concept of this type was in the mind of David Hume, the moral philosopher, who believed that the right to own private property is the basis for the modern concept of justice in morals.

Nor is it surprising to discover that two of history's leading exponents of the Welfare State concept found it necessary to denounce this moral code completely. Marx said: "Religion is the opium of the people." And Lenin said: "Any religious idea, any idea of a 'good God' . . . is an abominably nasty thing." Of course they would have to say these things about religious beliefs. This is because the moral code of these great religions, as we have seen, strikes at the very heart of their immoral economic scheme. Not only does their Welfare State scheme deny the moral right to private property, but it also denies other underlying bases of the moral code, as we shall see.

Moral Right to Work and to Have

Stealing and coveting are condemned in the Decalogue as violations of the basic moral code. It follows, then, that the concepts of stealing and coveting presume the right to private property, which then automatically becomes an implied part of the basic moral code. But where does private property come from?

Private property comes from what one has saved out of what he has produced, or has earned as a productive employee of another person. One may also, of course, obtain private property through gifts and inheritances; but in the absence of theft, precluded by this moral code, gifts come from those who have produced or earned what is given. So the right of private property, and also the right to have whatever one has produced or earned, underlies the admonitions in the Decalogue about stealing and coveting. Nobody has the moral right to take by force from the producer anything he has produced or earned, for any purpose whatsoever—even for a good purpose, as he thinks of it.

If one is free to have what he has produced and earned, it then follows that he also has the moral right to be free to choose his work. He should be free to choose his work, that is, so long as he does not violate the moral code by using in his productive efforts the property of another person through theft or trespass. Otherwise he is free to work as he will, at what he will, and to change his work when he will. Nobody has the moral right to force him to work when he does not choose to do so, or to force him to remain idle when he wishes to work, or to force him to work at a certain job when he wishes to work at some other available job. The belief of the master that his judgment is superior to that of the slave or vassal, and that control is "for his own good," is not a moral justification for the idea of the Welfare State.

We are told that some misdoings occurred in a Garden of Eden, which signify the evil in man. And I would concede that no mortal man is totally wise and good. But it is my belief that people generally, up and down the road, are intuitively and predominantly moral. By this I mean that if persons are confronted with a clear and simple decision involving basic morals, most of us will conduct ourselves morally. Almost everyone, without being a learned scholar of moral philosophy, seems to have a sort of innate sense of what is right, and tends to do what is moral *unless and until he becomes confused by circumstances which obscure the moral issue that is involved.*

Immorality Is News

The content of many magazines and newspapers with widespread circulations would seem to contradict my belief that most people are moral most of the time. They headline impressive and unusual events on the seamy side of life, which might lead one to believe that these events are characteristic of everyday human affairs. It is to be noted, however, that their content is in sharp contrast to the local, hometown daily or weekly with its emphasis on the folksy reports of the comings and goings of friends. Why the difference? Those with large circulations find that the common denominator of news interest in their audience is events on the rare, seamy side of life; widely scattered millions are not interested in knowing that in Centerville, Sally attended Susie's birthday party last Tuesday.

It is the rarity of evil conduct that makes it impressive news for millions. Papers report the event of yesterday's murder, theft, or assault, together with the name, address, age, marital status, religious affiliation, and other descriptive features of the guilty party because these are the events of the day that are unusual enough to be newsworthy. What would be the demand for a newspaper which published all the names and identifications of all the persons who yesterday failed to murder, steal, or assault? If it were as rare for persons to act morally as it is now rare for them to act immorally, the then rare instances of moral conduct would presumably become the news of the day. So we may conclude that evil is news because it is so rare, that being moral is not news because it is so prevalent.

But does not this still prove the dominance of evil in persons? Or, since magazines and newspapers print what finds a ready readership in the market, does not that prove the evilness of those who read of evil? I believe not. It is more like the millions who attend zoos, and view with fascination the monkeys and the snakes; these spectators are not themselves monkeys or snakes nor do they want to be; they are merely expressing an interest in the unusual, without envy. Do not most of us read of a bank robbery or a fire without wishing to be robbers or arsonists?

What else dominates the newspaper space, and gives us our dominant impressions about the quality of persons outside our circle of immediate personal acquaintance? It is mostly about the problems of political power, about those who have power or are grasping for power, diluted with a little about those who are fighting against power. Lord Acton said: "Power tends to corrupt, and absolute power corrupts absolutely." This dictum seems to be true, as history has proved and is proving over and over again. So we can then translate it into a description of much of the news of the day: News is heavily loaded with items about persons who, as Lord Acton said, are either corrupt or are in the process of becoming more corrupt.

If one is not careful in exposing himself to the daily news—if he fails to keep his balance and forgets how it contrasts with all those persons who comprise his family, his neighbors, his business associates, and his friends—he is likely to conclude falsely that people are predominantly immoral. This poses a serious problem for historians and historical novelists to the extent that their source of information is the news of a former day—especially if they do not interpret it with caution.

To Steal or Not To Steal

As a means of specifically verifying my impression about the basic, intuitive morality of persons, I would pose this test of three questions:

1. Would you steal your neighbor's cow to provide for your present needs? Would you steal it for any need reasonably within your expectation or comprehension? It should be remembered that, instead of stealing his cow, you may explore with your neighbor the possible solution to your case of need; you might arrange to do some sort of work for him, or to borrow from him for later repayment, or perhaps even plead with him for an outright gift.

2. Would you steal your neighbor's cow to provide for a known case of another neighbor's need?

3. Would you try to induce a third party to do the stealing of the cow, to be given to this needy neighbor? And do you believe that you would likely succeed in inducing him to engage in the theft?

I believe that the almost universal answer to all these questions would be: "No." Yet the facts of the case are that all of us are participating in theft every day. How? By supporting the actions of the collective agent which does the stealing as part of the Welfare State program already far advanced in the United States. By this device, Peter is robbed to "benefit" Paul, with the acquiescence if not the active support of all of us as taxpayers and citizens. We not only participate in the stealing—and share in the division of the loot—but as its victims we also meekly submit to the thievery.

Isn't it a strange thing that if you select any three fundamentally moral persons and combine them into a collective for the doing of good, they are liable at once to become three immoral persons in their collective activities? The moral principles with which they seem to be intuitively endowed are somehow lost in the confusing processes of the collective. None of the three would steal the cow from one of his fellow members as an individual, but collectively they all steal cows from each other. The reason is, I believe, that the Welfare State—a confusing collective device which is believed by many to be moral and righteous—has been falsely labeled. This false label has caused the belief that the Welfare State can do no wrong, that it cannot commit immoral acts, especially if those acts are approved or tolerated by more than half of the people, "democratically."

This sidetracking of moral conduct is like the belief of an earlier day: The king can do no wrong. In its place we have now substituted this belief: The majority can do no wrong. It is as though one were to assert that a sheep which has been killed by a pack of wolves is not really dead, provided that more than half of the wolves have participated in the killing. All these excuses for immoral conduct are, of course, nonsense. They are nonsense when tested against the basic moral code of the five postulates. Thievery is thievery, whether done by one person alone or by many in a pack, or by one who has been selected by the members of the pack as their agent.

"Thou Shalt Not Steal, Except . . . "

It seems that wherever the Welfare State is involved, the moral precept, "Thou shalt not steal," becomes altered to say: "Thou shalt not steal, except for what thou deemest to be a worthy cause, where thou thinkest that thou canst use the loot for a better purpose than wouldst the victim of the theft."

And the precept about covetousness, under the administration of the Welfare State, seems to become: "Thou shalt not covet, except what thou wouldst have from thy neighbor who owns it."

Both of these alterations of the Decalogue result in complete abrogation of the two moral admonitions—theft and covetousness—which deal directly with economic matters. Not even the motto, "In God we trust," stamped by the government on money taken by force in violation of the Decalogue to pay for the various programs of the Welfare State, can transform this immoral act into a moral one.

Herein lies the principal moral and economic danger facing us in these critical times: Many of us, albeit with good intentions but in a hurry to do good because of the urgency of the occasion, have become victims of moral schizophrenia. While we are good and righteous persons in our individual conduct in our home community and in our basic moral code, we have become thieves and coveters in the collective activities of the Welfare State in which we participate and which many of us extol.

Typical of our times is what usually happens when there is a major catastrophe, destroying private property or injuring many persons. The news circulates, and generates widespread sympathy for the victims. So what is done about it? Through the mechanisms of the collective, the good intentions take the form of reaching into the other fellow's pocket for the money with which to make a gift. The Decalogue says, in effect: "Reach into your *own* pocket—not into your neighbor's pocket—to finance your acts of compassion; good cannot be done with the loot that comes from theft." The pickpocket, in other words, is a thief even though he puts the proceeds in the collection box on Sunday, or uses it to buy bread for the poor. Being an involuntary Good Samaritan is a contradiction in terms.

When thievery is resorted to for the means with which to do good, compassion is killed. Those who would do good with the loot then lose their capacity for self-reliance, the same as a thief's self-reliance atrophies rapidly when he subsists on food that is stolen. And those who are repeatedly robbed of their property simultaneously lose their capacity for compassion. The chronic victims of robbery are under great temptation to join the gang and share in the loot. They come to feel that the voluntary way of life will no longer suffice for needs; that to subsist, they must rob and be robbed. They abhor violence, of course, but approve of robbing by "peaceful means." It is this peculiar immoral distinction which many try to draw between the Welfare State of Russia and that of Britain: The Russian brand of violence, they believe, is bad; that of Britain, good. This version of an altered Commandment would be: "Thou shalt not steal, except from nonresisting victims."

Under the Welfare State, this process of theft has spread from its use in alleviating catastrophe, to anticipating catastrophe, to conjuring up catastrophe, to the "need" for luxuries for those who have them not. The acceptance of the practice of thus violating the Decalogue has become so widespread that if the Sermon on the Mount were to appear in our day in the form of an address or publication, it would most likely be scorned as "reactionary, and not objective on the realistic problems of the day." Forgotten, it seems, by many who so much admire Christ, is the fact that he did not resort to theft in acquiring the means of his material benefactions. Nor did he advocate theft for any purpose—even for those uses most dear to his beliefs.

Progress of Moral Decay

Violation of the two economic Commandments—theft and covetousness—under the program of the Welfare State, will spread to the other Commandments; it will destroy faith in, and observance of, our entire basic moral code. We have seen this happen in many countries. It seems to have been happening here. We note how immorality, as tested by the two economic Commandments, has spread in high places to such an extent that violations of all other parts of the Decalogue and of the Golden Rule have become accepted as commonplace—even proper and worthy of emulation.

And what about the effectiveness of a crime investigation conducted under a Welfare State government? We may question the presumed capability of such a government—as distinct from certain investigators who are admittedly moral individuals—to judge these moral issues. We may also question the wisdom of bothering to investigate the picayune amounts of private gambling, willingly engaged in by the participants with their own money, when untold billions are being taken from the people repeatedly by the investigating agent to finance its own immoral program. This is a certain loss, not even a gamble.

Once a right to collective looting has been substituted for the right of each person to have whatever he has produced, it is not at all surprising to find the official dispensers deciding that it is right for them to loot the loot—for a "worthy" purpose, of course. Then we have the loot used by the insiders to buy votes so that they may stay in power; we have political pork barrels and lobbying for the contents; we have political patronage for political loyalty—even for loyalty to immoral conduct; we have all sorts of gifts and personal favors given to political friends and bribes for the opportunity to do privileged business with those who hold and dispense the loot. Why not? If it is right to loot, it is also right to loot the loot. If the latter is wrong, so also is the former.

If we are to accept Lord Acton's axiom about the corrupting effect of power—and also the reasoning of Professor Hayek in his book, *The Road to Serfdom*, about why the worst get to the top in a Welfare State—then corruption and low moral standards in high political places should not be surprising. But when the citizens come more and more to laugh and joke about it, rather than to remove the crown of power and dismantle the throne, a nation is well on its way to moral rot, reminiscent of the fall of the Roman Empire and others.

Nor should we be surprised that there is some juvenile delinquency where adult delinquency is so rampant, and where the absence of any basic moral code among adults precludes even the possibility of their effectively teaching a moral code that will prevent delinquency in the young. If, as adults, we practice collective thievery through the Welfare State, and advocate it as right and good, how can we question the logic of the youths who likewise form gangs and rob the candy store? If demonstration is the best teacher, we adults must start with the practice of morality ourselves, rather than hiring some presumed specialist to study the causes of similar conduct among the youngsters; their conduct is the symptom, not the disease.

Thievery and covetousness will persist and grow, and the basic morals of ourselves, our children, and our children's children will continue to deteriorate unless we destroy the virus of immorality that is embedded in the concept of the Welfare State; unless we come to understand how the moral code of individual conduct must apply also to collective conduct, because the collective is composed solely of individuals. Moral individual conduct cannot persist in the face of collective immorality under the Welfare State program. One side or the other of the double standard of morals will have to be surrendered.

Appendix: The Welfare State Idea

The concept of the Welfare State appears in our everyday life in the form of a long list of labels and programs such as: Social Security; parity or fair prices; reasonable profits; the living wage; the TVA, MVA, CVA; Federal aid to states, to education, to bankrupt corporations; and so on.

But all these names and details of the Welfare State program tend only to obscure its essential nature. They are well-sounding labels for a laudable objective—the relief of distressing need, prevention of starvation, and the like. But how best are starvation and distress to be prevented? It is good, too, that prices, profits, and wages be fair and equitable. But what is to be the test of fairness and equity? Laudable objectives alone do not assure the success of any program; a fair appraisal of the program must include an analysis of the means of its attainment.

The Welfare State is a name that has been substituted as a more acceptable one for communism-socialism wherever, as in the United States, these names are in general disrepute.

The Welfare State plan, viewed in full bloom of completeness, is one where the state prohibits the individual from having any right of choice in the conditions and place of his work; it takes ownership of the product of his labor; it prohibits private property. All these are done ostensibly to help those whose rights have been taken over by the Welfare State.

But these characteristics of controlled employment and confiscation of income are not those used in promotion of the idea of the Welfare State. What are usually advertised, instead, are the "benefits" of the Welfare State—the grants of food and housing and whatnot—which the state "gives" to the people. But all these "benefits" are merely the other side of the forfeited rights to choose one's own occupation and to keep whatever one is able to produce. In the same sense that the Welfare State grants benefits, the slavemaster grants to his slaves certain allotments of food and other economic goods. In fact, slavery might be described as just another form of Welfare State, because of its likeness in restrictions and "benefits."

Yet the state, as such, produces nothing with which to supply these "benefits." Persons produce everything which the Welfare State takes, before it gives some back as "benefits"; but in the process, the bureaucracy takes its cut. Only by thus confiscating what persons have produced can the Welfare State "satisfy the needs of the people." So, the necessary and essential idea of the Welfare State is to control the economic actions of the vassals of the state, to take from producers what they produce, and to prevent their ever being able to attain economic independence from the state and from their fellow men through ownership of property.

To whatever extent an individual is still allowed freedom in any of these respects while living under a government like the present one in the United States, then to that extent the development of the program of the Welfare State is as yet not fully completed. Or perhaps it is an instance of a temporary grant of freedom by the

Welfare State such as when a master allows his slave a day off from work to spend as he likes; but the person who is permitted some freedom by the Welfare State is still a vassal of that state just as a slave is still a slave on his day off from work.

Part Five

Personal Practice

Leonard Read's bimonthly *Notes from FEE* along with the score or more of books by him between 1954 and 1982 dealt extensively with the "methodology" of freedom. In other words, he was deeply concerned with the personal practice of the philosophy of freedom. Freedom to him was very much a do-it-yourself project—a process of improving society by means of self-improvement. Set an example that others may choose to follow.

Such is the theme of his short essay in this selection as well as the one by Dr. Hans Sennholz and the ever-popular statements by Davy Crockett and Albert Jay Nock.

10

Looking Out for Yourself

by Leonard E. Read

From a 1956 college commencement address.

First, may I offer you hearty and well deserved congratulations on completing the formal, institutional phase of your education. And I especially offer you best wishes for the next and most important phase of your education—that which is to come under your own management. For assuredly, graduates of this splendid Institute will avoid an all too common error—the notion that the beginning of earning is the end of learning!

It is not at all improbable that you have, until now, been so engrossed in technical and other formal educational pursuits, that you have given but scant thought to the educational program you must resolve for yourself, beginning tomorrow. I would like to present for your consideration some of the problems I foresee for you, issues with which students of specialized subjects may not be too familiar.

Unless you are alerted, or are different from most of the folks I know, you can easily remain unaware of the two opposed ways of life that will be contesting for your attention and support in the years ahead. One of these ways—the collectivistic—has by far the most numerous adherents. Indeed, you will be fortunate if you find even a few individuals who harbor no collectivism whatever. Collectivism is easy enough to identify when it comes plainly tagged as socialism, communism, Fabianism, Nazism, the Welfare State, the planned economy, or state interventionism. But one has to be sharply discriminating to discern it when it is untagged or concealed; when it is offered as proper fare by so-called conservative political parties; when it is endorsed by many high-ranking business leaders and their organizations; or when it is urged upon you by your best friends.

Collectivism is a system or idea which holds that the collective—as distinguished from the individual—is what counts. Individual hopes, aspirations, and needs are subordinated to what is termed "the collective good." Practically, no such system can be implemented unless some person or set of persons interprets what "the collective good" is. Since it is impossible to obtain unanimous and voluntary agreements to these interpretations, they have to be enforced—and enforcement requires a police arrangement which in turn dominates the lives of all persons embraced by the collective. Implicit in all authoritarian systems are wage and price controls, dictation as to what will be produced and distributed, and by whom.

Russia is the world's most pronounced example, but here at home we see the same thing rearing its head in the form of rent control, Valley Authorities, public housing, parity prices, acreage allotments, union monopoly, federal subsidies of every description, federal subventions to states and cities and districts, governmental foreign-aid programs, import quotas, tariffs, manipulation of money, such as the monetization of debt, and so forth.

However, it is more or less idle for me to dwell on what I believe to be error. As has been well repeated over and over again, "It is better to light a candle than to curse the darkness." A much sounder approach is to displace the wrong by advancing the right, to argue positively instead of negatively. With this in mind, I should like to take sides in the ideological conflict of our times and commend to your attention the way of life which is the opposite of collectivism. This way of life, also, has numerous labels, but I'm going to give it a simple and descriptive name, "Looking Out for Yourself." That's about as opposite as you can get from having the government looking out for you.

A Positive Approach

Now there's a lot more to this looking-out-for-yourself philosophy than first meets the eye. To the unreflective person—to the victim of clichés and catch phrases—it will suggest a life of non-cooperation, greed, the law of the jungle, and no concern for the well-being of others. But, be not deceived. If you intelligently look out for yourself, you will thereby follow the way of life most valuable to others.

Perhaps you will better understand this idea when I explain why there isn't anyone on earth you can constructively control except yourself. Control can be divided into two types, the destructive and the creative. It is simple enough to control others destructively. Little intellectual achievement is required to restrain others, to inhibit their actions, to destroy their lives. There are all sorts of ways to get on the backs of others and hinder them in their creative actions. But the hindering type of control is quite different from the helping type. The hindering type rests primarily and ultimately on the application of brute or physical force.

The Limited Role of Force

Now brute or physical force is all right if confined to its proper sphere—that is, restraining and inhibiting destructive actions such as violence, fraud, misrepresentation, and predation against peaceful persons. Broadly speaking, this is the logical function of government. In sound theory, government should use its police powers only to do for all of us equally that which each of us has a moral right to do for himself in defense of his life, liberty, and property. It should apply physical force only defensively in order to repel that which is evil and unjust.

It should be clearly understood that brute, physical, or police force cannot constructively help anyone. It can give only a negative assist by clearing the obstacles from the road to opportunity. No person, nor any set of persons, can physically force anyone to invent, to discover, to create. Let us face this fact: One can have no control whatever over any other person creatively. We are indeed fortunate if we have very much control even over ourselves creatively. In any event, such creative control as any of us possesses is confined strictly and exclusively to self.

Creatively, man has no control over others, no power over others, except the power of attraction; and even then, it is the other person who decides upon and determines the degree of attraction. This is a God-bestowed limitation on all men for which we should be forever grateful. I, at least, am pleased that others cannot *compel* me to accept as eternal verities that which they claim to know. And I am even more pleased that I cannot force my opinions and beliefs upon others.

The Power of Attraction

The power of attraction is always and forever a subjective judgment! One may be attractive to none, to a few, to many. Figuratively, others look us over and decide for themselves whether or not we have anything worth their consideration. After all these years of schooling, you fully realize that no teacher is ever self-designated. It has always been you who decided what, if anything, you learned from your teachers. Or, to use a more obvious example, it is the person with the receiving set who does the tuning in—it is never the broadcaster.

Put it this way: I can help you in a material sense only if I have money to lend or give to you, or goods and services to exchange with you. I cannot help you materially if I am a pauper. Intellectually, I can assist you if I possess understanding not yet yours. The ignorant can give us no help intellectually. Spiritually, I can be of value to you only if I am in possession of insights which you have not yet experienced. Materially, intellectually, and spiritually, I am limited as to what I can do for any other person by what I have to give, by how well I have looked out for myself in these areas.

Once we have grasped the idea that the best way to help others is first to look out for ourselves, we should next consider how important it is that we do help others. I would like to emphasize the point that each of us, if self-interest be interpreted accurately, has a vested interest in the material, intellectual, and spiritual well-being of others; that our very existence depends on others.

A Society of Specialists

To appreciate the extent of our dependence on others, we need but realize that we are living in the most specialized, the most advanced division-of-labor, the most removed-from-self-subsistence society in all of recorded history.

For example, you will discover, as you take up your highly specialized tasks, that someone else will be growing, processing, and delivering your food, that someone else will be making your clothing, building your home, providing your transportation, supplying your heat, and making available to you most of the new knowledge you acquire. Indeed, you will discover that individuals from all over this earth will be at your service, willingly exchanging their millions of specialties for your own single specialty. You will discover that you will consume in a single day that which you could not possibly produce solely by yourself in thousands of years. You will see about you a release and exchange of creative energies so fabulous that no living man can trace or diagnose the miracle. You will, for instance, pick up the receiver of a telephone, and instantly there will flow to your personal service the creative energies of Alexander Graham Bell—of tens of thousands of metallurgists, engineers, scientists, operators, linesmen—a complex of creative energies flowing through space and time in order that you may talk to your parents or friends in a matter of seconds.

No one of us can exist without these others. And I repeat, each of us has a vested and vital interest in the creative energies of other people and in the uninhibited exchange of their services, ideas, and insights. We must, if we would intelligently look out for ourselves, see to it as best we can that these others be free of private or political marauders, interventionists, and parasites. Any inhibition to their creative lives is opposed to your and my personal interests, and we err and do not look out for ourselves if we sanction or fail to oppose such debasement. And further, it is incumbent upon all of us to rise as far as we can in our own intellectual and spiritual statures so that these others, on whom we depend, may find something in turn to draw from us.

There is another point about this highly specialized society which deserves your reflection. You men and women, highly trained as specialists yourselves, represent the cream of this year's crop. Tomorrow, you will enter a society in which there will be millions of specialists, the cream of numerous former crops. I hope you will not emulate so many of them who attend only to their own specialties and little else beyond acquiring wealth and entertainment. Perhaps the most dangerous trend of our times is this: Specialists—the cream of the crop in intellectual and spiritual potentialities—who, by attending only to their diverse specializations, leave to the skim milk of the crop the vital problems of man's proper relationships to man.

Danger of Overspecialization

Specialization has its unquestioned blessings. But there is always the danger, which we are now witnessing, of its taking off like spokes from the hub of a wheel, on and on with no regard to boundary or periphery, with each specialist heading into an ever-advancing remoteness, into an atomistic world of his own, always widening his distance from others, losing social cohesiveness with society disintegrating as each of us loses integration with others, with communication between specialists becoming more and more impossible, with nearly all specialists "too busy" to read, study, and meditate on the general problems of man's proper relationships to man. When these trends characterize a society, that society isn't merely doomed to collapse; it is destined to explode! If you would look out for yourself—and thus for others—you will by example and precept do your part in reversing such trends.

In order that I be not misunderstood, I repeat that specialization has its unquestioned blessings. Specialization, when practiced by whole men, by those who reflect on the meaning of life, by those who have an acquaintance with the humanities, in a society where creative energies are uninhibited, is the road to material wealth—which can, in turn, lead to intellectual and spiritual wealth. But while specialization is the means to wealth, let us not think of material wealth as an end in itself. Material wealth, like specialization, is only the means to higher ends—intellectual and spiritual wealth.

Wealth Can Free Man for Higher Aims

It seems to me that if material wealth has any moral purpose at all, it is to free man from the restrictions which are imposed by a subsistence level of living; for when one has to labor in the rice paddies from sunrise to sunset merely to eke out an animal existence, he doesn't stand much chance of evolving and developing those numerous potentialities peculiar to his own person. But wealth is not something to be pursued for wealth's sake or merely for luxuries, or quick retirement, or for shirking the problems of life. Material wealth, morally speaking, is but the means to free us from lower employments so that we may labor more industriously at higher employments, that we may develop more fully the life of the intellect and of the spirit. Material wealth is but a tool to help us develop our God-given faculties of intellect and spirit.

And now, a word of counsel. The market place is in high-pitched competition for your specialized services, and the emoluments being offered are relatively high. This may make the future look extraordinarily promising to you. And it can be promising if you don't become isolated in your own specializations. There are many brilliant but lost specialists in industry today, persons who cannot be promoted into higher positions because of a narrowness in their scope. They lack an interest in the problems of others on whom they depend, and an understanding of the society in which it is their lot to live.

Broadening One's Perspective

Broadening one's scope, continuing one's education into other than one's own specialty, is not a dismal but a glorious prospect. It can be the very zest of life. Certainly, it is a well-known fact that any specialist, be he writer, painter, cook, or engineer, is a better specialist if there be breadth in his understanding, if he be an integrated person, if he has balanced judgments as to right and wrong principles in man's relationships to man.

The deviltry going on in the world today is not primarily caused by criminals. The truly malevolent persons are too few in number to account for our wars and the continuing accumulation of vast armaments between major conflicts. The thoroughly evil persons among us are not numerous enough to account for all the racial and national hatreds and prejudices, for labor violence, for the growing belief that the honest fruits of one's labor no longer belong to the earner, for restrictions on the exchange of goods and services, and for the many other collectivistic inanities and horrors. These things are not the doings of criminals. They originate mostly with the well-intentioned, those who wish to do good to others but who, lacking personal means, thoughtlessly see no harm in employing police establishments to impose their brand of good on the rest of us, to use the fruits of other persons' labor to satisfy their own charitable instincts.

God bless you in your chosen pursuits, but I implore you not to specialize to the exclusion of your role as good citizens. Don't leave us and yourselves to the mercy of political parasites, those who would try to act the part of God, those who would cast us all in their immature little images. If you would effectively look out for yourselves and thus for others, if you would have a society in which your specializations are to have meaning for you and for your fellow men, if you would realize the possibilities in your own individual creations, you will attend to the perfection of that society. And you will best do this by the perfection of yourselves, not only as skilled specialists but also as accomplished expositors of the looking-out-for-yourself philosophy.

11

Different Yardsticks

by Hans F. Sennholz

Dr. Sennholz is Professor of Economics at Grove City College, Pennsylvania. He is the author of several books and numerous articles, many of which have appeared in The Freeman. *He is a trustee of FEE and a regular seminar lecturer. His article was first published in December 1956, but is an ever-timely caution concerning the distinction between personal and political behavior.*

The Christian law of neighborly love is an unbending rule of individual conduct, a rule without flexibility or loopholes for perverting interpretation. It is a basic maxim for all social cooperation and peaceful human coexistence. Indeed, it is an indispensable cornerstone of every civilization.

And yet we have been unwittingly and gradually chiseling away its shape and strength until it has become a small stump that no longer is capable of supporting social life and interhuman relations.

The law of love still underlies most of our direct man-to-man relations. In our family lives we practice, or at least endeavor to practice, this commandment. In our direct relations with our neighbor we inflict no harm, or at least endeavor to inflict no harm, on him and his family. A friendly neighborly relationship is still more frequent than a malicious one. In all our social contacts, be they in our economic associations or any other casual acquaintance, we basically respect our fellow man's rights and liberty.

But we are different men as soon as we take part in the body politic. Here there is no room for the law of neighborly love. Acting in political concert we act in a way no conscientious man would dream of acting in direct interhuman relations. We leave no room for God in our political lives.

Take the following examples:

As individuals we do not think of exacting, through violence or threat of violence, any part of our neighbor's wealth or income; but in our political lives we feel free to exact most of his income through heavy tax levies and control his wealth through a multiplicity of economic regulations.

As parents we do not think of coercing our neighbor to contribute funds to the education of our children; as members of the body politic we resort to taxation in order to coerce him to contribute to our children's education so that they may have "free public education" and we may be "freed" from all or part of our own obligations.

We do not think of envying and pilfering our neighbor of his savings, his pension, and income from a life insurance policy; but as political beings we shatter their values through government policies of inflation and monetary depreciation.

We do not think of begrudging his widow and orphans their inheritance and do not coerce them to institute us as their coheirs; as members of the body politic we may force them to turn over half or more of their inheritance to us.

Two Different Yardsticks

As individuals we do not think of coercing our fellow men in other parts of the Union to help us in our local economic endeavors; as political beings we coerce them to assist us in our own selfish ends through Federal aid and other government contributions.

If evil men were to encroach upon our neighbor and extort all or part of his property or income, or in any other way oppress him, we courageously may come to his assistance. If he should hurt or even kill one of his transgressors, we may acquit him from criminal guilt for having acted in self-defense.

If he should hurt or kill our own "duly authorized representative" who was empowered to exact a part of our neighbor's income or "control" his wealth for our own selfish ends, we would condemn him and our wrath and revenge would thrust him into penitentiaries or death chambers.

We measure our deeds and actions with two different yardsticks of morality. We are quick and severe in the condemnation of the misdeeds our neighbor commits. But we fail to judge at all or at least with the same severity our own actions through the body politic.

We condemn a neighbor for deceit, theft, robbery, and other crimes against his fellow men; but we fail to judge ourselves for confiscatory taxation, nationalization, and seizures of private industries by government, our political instrument.

Two Souls in Our Breasts

We condemn a man for his disregard of promises, contracts, and agreements and endeavor to hold him to his contractual obligations through court action and other legal means at our disposal. But we readily acquiesce in government policies that disregard promises, or tear up official charters and international agreements. We may even sympathize with governments conducting such lawless policies and condemn those who are hurt and finally act in self-defense.

Indeed there are two souls in our breasts, one that seeks and fears God, the other that denies the very presence of God. Man has paid and is still paying a tremendous price for his rejection of the Christian law of neighborly love in the ever-expanding sphere of political action. The price is paid in the shape of slavery, war, and disaster.

12

Not Yours To Give

by Davy Crockett

This story by and about Davy Crockett is taken from The Life of
Colonel David Crockett, *compiled by Edward S. Ellis (Philadelphia; Porter & Coates, 1884).*

*Holders of political office are but reflections of the dominant
leadership—good or bad—among the electorate. Horatio Bunce is
a striking example of responsible citizenship. Were his kind to
multiply we would see many new faces in public office; or, as in
the case of Davy Crockett, a new Crockett.*

One day in the House of Representatives, a bill was taken
up appropriating money for the benefit of a widow of a
distinguished naval officer. Several beautiful speeches had
been made in its support. The Speaker was just about to put the
question when Crockett arose:

"Mr. Speaker—I have as much respect for the memory of the
deceased, and as much sympathy for the sufferings of the living, if
suffering there be, as any man in this House, but we must not
permit our respect for the dead or our sympathy for a part of the
living to lead us into an act of injustice to the balance of the living.
I will not go into an argument to prove that Congress has no
power to appropriate this money as an act of charity. Every
member upon this floor knows it. We have the right, as individuals, to give away as much of our own money as we please in
charity; but as members of Congress we have no right so to
appropriate a dollar of the public money. Some eloquent appeals
have been made to us upon the ground that it is a debt due the

118

deceased. Mr. Speaker, the deceased lived long after the close of the war; he was in office to the day of his death, and I have never heard that the government was in arrears to him.

"Every man in this House knows it is not a debt. We cannot, without the grossest corruption, appropriate this money as the payment of a debt. We have not the semblance of authority to appropriate it as a charity. Mr. Speaker, I have said we have the right to give as much money of our own as we please. I am the poorest man on this floor. I cannot vote for this bill, but I will give one week's pay to the object, and if every member of Congress will do the same, it will amount to more than the bill asks."

He took his seat. Nobody replied. The bill was put upon its passage, and, instead of passing unanimously, as was generally supposed, and as, no doubt, it would, but for that speech, it received but few votes, and, of course, was lost.

Later, when asked by a friend why he had opposed the appropriation, Crockett gave this explanation:

"Several years ago I was one evening standing on the steps of the Capitol with some other members of Congress, when our attention was attracted by a great light over in Georgetown. It was evidently a large fire. We jumped into a hack and drove over as fast as we could. In spite of all that could be done, many houses were burned and many families made houseless, and, besides, some of them had lost all but the clothes they had on. The weather was very cold, and when I saw so many women and children suffering, I felt that something ought to be done for them. The next morning a bill was introduced appropriating $20,000 for their relief. We put aside all other business and rushed it through as soon as it could be done.

"The next summer, when it began to be time to think about the election, I concluded I would take a scout around among the boys of my district. I had no opposition there, but, as the election was some time off, I did not know what might turn up. When riding one day in a part of my district in which I was more of a stranger than any other, I saw a man in a field plowing and coming toward the road. I gauged my gait so that we should meet as he came to the fence. As he came up, I spoke to the man. He replied politely, but, as I thought, rather coldly.

"I began: 'Well, friend, I am one of those unfortunate beings called candidates, and—'

"'Yes, I know you; you are Colonel Crockett. I have seen you once before, and voted for you the last time you were elected. I suppose you are out electioneering now, but you had better not waste your time or mine. I shall not vote for you again.'

"This was a sockdolager . . . I begged him to tell me what was the matter.

"'Well, Colonel, it is hardly worth-while to waste time or words upon it. I do not see how it can be mended, but you gave a vote last winter which shows that either you have not capacity to understand the Constitution, or that you are wanting in the honesty and firmness to be guided by it. In either case you are not the man to represent me. But I beg your pardon for expressing it in that way. I did not intend to avail myself of the privilege of the constituent to speak plainly to a candidate for the purpose of insulting or wounding you. I intend by it only to say that your understanding of the Constitution is very different from mine; and I will say to you what, but for my rudeness, I should not have said, that I believe you to be honest. . . . But an understanding of the Constitution different from mine I cannot overlook, because the Constitution, to be worth anything, must be held sacred, and rigidly observed in all its provisions. The man who wields power and misinterprets it is the more dangerous the more honest he is.'

"'I admit the truth of all you say, but there must be some mistake about it, for I do not remember that I gave any vote last winter upon any constitutional question.'

"'No, Colonel, there's no mistake. Though I live here in the backwoods and seldom go from home, I take the papers from Washington and read very carefully all the proceedings of Congress. My papers say that last winter you voted for a bill to appropriate $20,000 to some sufferers by a fire in Georgetown. Is that true?'

"'Well, my friend; I may as well own up. You have got me there. But certainly nobody will complain that a great and rich country like ours should give the insignificant sum of $20,000 to relieve its suffering women and children, particularly with a full and overflowing Treasury, and I am sure, if you had been there, you would have done just as I did.'

"'It is not the amount, Colonel, that I complain of; it is the principle. In the first place, the government ought to have in the Treasury no more than enough for its legitimate purposes. But that has nothing to do with the question. The power of collecting and disbursing money at pleasure is the most dangerous power that can be intrusted to man, particularly under our system of collecting revenue by a tariff, which reaches every man in the country, no matter how poor he may be, and the poorer he is the more he pays in proportion to his means. What is worse, it presses upon him without his knowledge where the weight centers, for there is not a man in the United States who can ever guess how much he pays to the government. So you see, that while you are contributing to relieve one, you are drawing it from thousands who are even worse off than he. If you had the right to give anything, the amount was simply a matter of discretion with you, and you had as much right to give $20,000,000 as $20,000. If you have the right to give to one, you have the right to give to all; and, as the Constitution neither defines charity nor stipulates the amount, you are at liberty to give to any and everything which you may believe, or profess to believe, is a charity, and to any amount you may think proper. You will very easily perceive what a wide door this would open for fraud and corruption and favoritism, on the one hand, and for robbing the people on the other. No, Colonel, Congress has no right to give charity. Individual members may give as much of their own money as they please, but they have no right to touch a dollar of the public money for that purpose. If twice as many houses had been burned in this county as in Georgetown, neither you nor any other member of Congress would have thought of appropriating a dollar for our relief. There are about two hundred and forty members of Congress. If they had shown their sympathy for the sufferers by contributing each one week's pay, it would have made over $13,000. There are plenty of wealthy men in and around Washington who could have given $20,000 without depriving themselves of even a luxury of life. The congressmen chose to keep their own money, which, if reports be true, some of them spend not very creditably; and the people of Washington, no doubt, applauded you for relieving them from the necessity of giving by giving what was not yours to give. The people have delegated to Congress, by the Constitution, the power to do certain things. To do these, it is authorized to collect and pay moneys, and for nothing else. Everything beyond this is usurpation, and a violation of the Constitution.

"'So you see, Colonel, you have violated the Constitution in what I consider a vital point. It is a precedent fraught with danger to the country, for when Congress once begins to stretch its power beyond the limits of the Constitution, there is no limit to it, and no security for the people. I have no doubt you acted honestly, but that does not make it any better, except as far as you are personally concerned, and you see that I cannot vote for you.'

"I tell you I felt streaked. I saw if I should have opposition, and this man should go to talking, he would set others to talking, and in that district I was a gone fawn-skin. I could not answer him, and the fact is, I was so fully convinced that he was right, I did not want to. But I must satisfy him, and I said to him:

"'Well, my friend, you hit the nail upon the head when you said I had not sense enough to understand the Constitution. I intended to be guided by it, and thought I had studied it fully. I have heard many speeches in Congress about the powers of Congress, but what you have said here at your plow has got more hard, sound sense in it than all the fine speeches I ever heard. If I had ever taken the view of it that you have, I would have put my head into the fire before I would have given that vote; and if you will forgive me and vote for me again, if I ever vote for another unconstitutional law I wish I may be shot.'

"He laughingly replied: 'Yes, Colonel, you have sworn to that once before, but I will trust you again upon one condition. You say that you are convinced that your vote was wrong. Your acknowledgment of it will do more good than beating you for it. If, as you go around the district, you will tell people about this vote, and that you are satisfied it was wrong, I will not only vote for you, but will do what I can to keep down opposition, and, perhaps, I may exert some little influence in that way.'

"'If I don't,' said I, 'I wish I may be shot; and to convince you that I am in earnest in what I say I will come back this way in a week or ten days, and if you will get up a gathering of the people, I will make a speech to them. Get up a barbecue, and I will pay for it.'

"'No, Colonel, we are not rich people in this section, but we have plenty of provisions to contribute for a barbecue, and some to spare for those who have none. The push of crops will be over in a few days, and we can then afford a day for a barbecue. This is Thursday; I will see to getting it up on Saturday week. Come to my house on Friday, and we will go together, and I promise you a very respectable crowd to see and hear you.'

"'Well, I will be here. But one thing more before I say good-by. I must know your name.'

"'My name is Bunce.'

"'Not Horatio Bunce?'

"'Yes.'

"'Well, Mr. Bunce, I never saw you before, though you say you have seen me, but I know you very well. I am glad I have met you, and very proud that I may hope to have you for my friend.'

"It was one of the luckiest hits of my life that I met him. He mingled but little with the public, but was widely known for his remarkable intelligence and incorruptible integrity, and for a heart brimful and running over with kindness and benevolence, which showed themselves not only in words but in acts. He was the oracle of the whole country around him, and his fame had extended far beyond the circle of his immediate acquaintance. Though I had never met him before, I had heard much of him, and but for this meeting it is very likely I should have had opposition, and had been beaten. One thing is very certain, no man could now stand up in that district under such a vote.

"At the appointed time I was at his house, having told our conversation to every crowd I had met, and to every man I stayed all night with, and I found that it gave the people an interest and a confidence in me stronger than I had ever seen manifested before.

"Though I was considerably fatigued when I reached his house, and, under ordinary circumstances, should have gone early to bed, I kept him up until midnight, talking about the principles and affairs of government, and got more real, true knowledge of them than I had got all my life before.

"I have known and seen much of him since, for I respect him— no, that is not the word—I reverence and love him more than any living man, and I go to see him two or three times every year; and I will tell you, sir, if every one who professes to be a Christian lived and acted and enjoyed it as he does, the religion of Christ would take the world by storm.

"But to return to my story. The next morning we went to the barbecue, and, to my surprise, found about a thousand men there. I met a good many whom I had not known before, and they and my friend introduced me around until I had got pretty well acquainted—at least, they all knew me.

"In due time notice was given that I would speak to them. They gathered up around a stand that had been erected. I opened my speech by saying:

"'Fellow-citizens—I present myself before you today feeling like a new man. My eyes have lately been opened to truths which ignorance or prejudice, or both, had heretofore hidden from my view. I feel that I can today offer you the ability to render you more valuable service than I have ever been able to render before. I am here today more for the purpose of acknowledging my error than to seek your votes. That I should make this acknowledgment is due to myself as well as to you. Whether you will vote for me is a matter for your consideration only.'

"I went on to tell them about the fire and my vote for the appropriation and then told them why I was satisfied it was wrong. I closed by saying:

"'And now, fellow-citizens, it remains only for me to tell you that most of the speech you have listened to with so much interest was simply a repetition of the arguments by which your neighbor, Mr. Bunce, convinced me of my error.

"'It is the best speech I ever made in my life, but he is entitled to the credit for it. And now I hope he is satisfied with his convert and that he will get up here and tell you so.'

"He came upon the stand and said:

"'Fellow-citizens—It affords me great pleasure to comply with the request of Colonel Crockett. I have always considered him a thoroughly honest man, and I am satisfied that he will faithfully perform all that he has promised you today.'

"He went down, and there went up from that crowd such a shout for Davy Crockett as his name never called forth before.

"I am not much given to tears, but I was taken with a choking then and felt some big drops rolling down my cheeks. And I tell you now that the remembrance of those few words spoken by such a man, and the honest, hearty shout they produced, is worth more to me than all the honors I have received and all the reputation I have ever made, or ever shall make, as a member of Congress.

"Now, sir," concluded Crockett, "you know why I made that speech yesterday.

"There is one thing now to which I will call your attention. You remember that I proposed to give a week's pay. There are in that House many very wealthy men—men who think nothing of spending a week's pay, or a dozen of them, for a dinner or a wine party when they have something to accomplish by it. Some of those same men made beautiful speeches upon the great debt of gratitude which the country owed the deceased—a debt which could not be paid by money—and the insignificance and worthlessness of money, particularly so insignificant a sum as $10,000, when weighed against the honor of the nation. Yet not one of them responded to my proposition. Money with them is nothing but trash when it is to come out of the people. But it is the one great thing for which most of them are striving, and many of them sacrifice honor, integrity, and justice to obtain it."

13

Isaiah's Job

by Albert Jay Nock

Albert Jay Nock (1870–1945) was editor of The Freeman *(1920–1924) and author of* Jefferson, Our Enemy The State, *and many other books and articles on the philosophy of government and human freedom. "Isaiah's Job" is extracted from Chapter 13 of his book,* Free Speech and Plain Language, *copyright 1937 by Albert Jay Nock. This book, now out of print, was published by William Morrow & Company, New York, and this extract is reprinted with their permission.*

"Isaiah's Job" is the best antidote we've found for a touch of the libertarian blues. It also offers excellent advice on how one may work most effectively for freedom. When "down in the dumps" or overcome by an impulse to "set the world straight," just give this another thoughtful reading.

One evening last autumn, I sat long hours with a European acquaintance while he expounded a politico-economic doctrine which seemed sound as a nut and in which I could find no defect. At the end, he said with great earnestness: "I have a mission to the masses. I feel that I am called to get the ear of the people. I shall devote the rest of my life to spreading my doctrine far and wide among the populace. What do you think?"

An embarrassing question in any case, and doubly so under the circumstances, because my acquaintance is a very learned man, one of the three or four really first-class minds that Europe produced in his generation; and naturally I, as one of the unlearned, was inclined to regard his lightest word with reverence amounting to awe. . . .

I referred him to the story of the prophet Isaiah. . . . I shall paraphrase the story in our common speech since it has to be pieced out from various sources. . . .

The prophet's career began at the end of King Uzziah's reign, say about 740 B.C. This reign was uncommonly long, almost half a century, and apparently prosperous. It was one of those prosperous reigns, however—like the reign of Marcus Aurelius at Rome, or the administration of Eubulus at Athens, or of Mr. Coolidge at Washington—where at the end the prosperity suddenly peters out and things go by the board with a resounding crash.

In the year of Uzziah's death, the Lord commissioned the prophet to go out and warn the people of the wrath to come. "Tell them what a worthless lot they are," He said. "Tell them what is wrong, and why, and what is going to happen unless they have a change of heart and straighten up. Don't mince matters. Make it clear that they are positively down to their last chance. Give it to them good and strong and keep on giving it to them. I suppose perhaps I ought to tell you," He added, "that it won't do any good. The official class and their intelligentsia will turn up their noses at you, and the masses will not even listen. They will all keep on in their own ways until they carry everything down to destruction, and you will probably be lucky if you get out with your life."

Isaiah had been very willing to take on the job—in fact, he had asked for it—but the prospect put a new face on the situation. It raised the obvious question: Why, if all that were so—if the enterprise were to be a failure from the start—was there any sense in starting it?

"Ah," the Lord said, "you do not get the point. There is a Remnant there that you know nothing about. They are obscure, unorganized, inarticulate, each one rubbing along as best he can. They need to be encouraged and braced up because when everything has gone completely to the dogs, they are the ones who will come back and build up a new society; and meanwhile, your preaching will reassure them and keep them hanging on. Your job is to take care of the Remnant, so be off now and set about it." . . .

What do we mean by the masses, and what by the Remnant?

As the word *masses* is commonly used, it suggests agglomera-

tions of poor and underprivileged people, laboring people, prole-
tarians. But it means nothing like that; it means simply the
majority. The mass-man is one who has neither the force of
intellect to apprehend the principles issuing in what we know as
the humane life, nor the force of character to adhere to those
principles steadily and strictly as laws of conduct; and because
such people make up the great, the overwhelming majority of
mankind, they are called collectively *the masses*. The line of
differentiation between the masses and the Remnant is set invari-
ably by quality, not by circumstance. The Remnant are those who
by force of intellect are able to apprehend these principles, and by
force of character are able, at least measurably, to cleave to them.
The masses are those who are unable to do either.

The picture which Isaiah presents of the Judean masses is most
unfavorable. In his view, the mass-man—be he high or be he
lowly, rich or poor, prince or pauper—gets off very badly. He
appears as not only weak-minded and weak-willed, but as by
consequence knavish, arrogant, grasping, dissipated, unprincipled,
unscrupulous. . . .

As things now stand, Isaiah's job seems rather to go begging.
Everyone with a message nowadays is, like my venerable European
friend, eager to take it to the masses. His first, last, and only
thought is of mass-acceptance and mass-approval. His great care is
to put his doctrine in such shape as will capture the masses'
attention and interest. . . .

The main trouble with this [mass-man approach] is its reaction
upon the mission itself. It necessitates an opportunist sophistica-
tion of one's doctrine, which profoundly alters its character and
reduces it to a mere placebo. If, say, you are a preacher, you wish
to attract as large a congregation as you can, which means an
appeal to the masses; and this, in turn, means adapting the terms
of your message to the order of intellect and character that the
masses exhibit. If you are an educator, say with a college on your
hands, you wish to get as many students as possible, and you
whittle down your requirements accordingly. If a writer, you aim
at getting many readers; if a publisher, many purchasers; if a
philosopher, many disciples; if a reformer, many converts; if a
musician, many auditors; and so on. But as we see on all sides, in
the realization of these several desires the prophetic message is so

heavily adulterated with trivialities, in every instance, that its effect on the masses is merely to harden them in their sins. Meanwhile, the Remnant, aware of this adulteration and of the desires that prompt it, turn their backs on the prophet and will have nothing to do with him or his message.

Isaiah, on the other hand, worked under no such disabilities. He preached to the masses only in the sense that he preached publicly. Anyone who liked might listen; anyone who liked might pass by. He knew that the Remnant would listen. . . .

The Remnant want only the best you have, whatever that may be. Give them that, and they are satisfied; you have nothing more to worry about. . . .

In a sense, nevertheless, as I have said, it is not a rewarding job. . . . A prophet of the Remnant will not grow purse-proud on the financial returns from his work, nor is it likely that he will get any great renown out of it. Isaiah's case was exceptional to this second rule, and there are others—but not many.

It may be thought, then, that while taking care of the Remnant is no doubt a good job, it is not an especially interesting job because it is as a rule so poorly paid. I have my doubts about this. There are other compensations to be got out of a job besides money and notoriety, and some of them seem substantial enough to be attractive. Many jobs which do not pay well are yet profoundly interesting, as, for instance, the job of the research student in the sciences is said to be; and the job of looking after the Remnant seems to me, as I have surveyed it for many years from my seat in the grandstand, to be as interesting as any that can be found in the world.

What chiefly makes it so, I think, is that in any given society the Remnant are always so largely an unknown quantity. You do not know, and will never know, more than two things about them. You can be sure of those—dead sure, as our phrase is—but you will never be able to make even a respectable guess at anything else. You do not know, and will never know, who the Remnant are, nor where they are, nor how many of them there are, nor what they are doing or will do. Two things you know, and no more: first, that they exist; second, that they will find you. Except for these two certainties, working for the Remnant means working in impenetrable darkness; and this, I should say, is just the condition calculated most effectively to pique the interest of any prophet who is properly gifted with the imagination, insight, and intellectual curiosity necessary to a successful pursuit of his trade.

The fascination—as well as the despair—of the historian, as he looks back upon Isaiah's Jewry, upon Plato's Athens, or upon Rome of the Antonines, is the hope of discovering and laying bare the "substratum of right-thinking and well-doing" which he knows must have existed somewhere in those societies because no kind of collective life can possibly go on without it. He finds tantalizing intimations of it here and there in many places, as in the Greek Anthology, in the scrapbook of Aulus Gellius, in the poems of Ausonius, and in the brief and touching tribute, *Bene merenti,* bestowed upon the unknown occupants of Roman tombs. But these are vague and fragmentary; they lead him nowhere in his search for some kind of measure of this substratum, but merely testify to what he already knew *a priori*—that the substratum did somewhere exist. Where it was, how substantial it was, what its power of self-assertion and resistance was—of all this they tell him nothing.

Similarly, when the historian of two thousand years hence, or two hundred years, looks over the available testimony to the quality of our civilization and tries to get any kind of clear, competent evidence concerning the substratum of right-thinking and well-doing which he knows must have been here, he will have a devil of a time finding it. When he has assembled all he can get and has made even a minimum allowance for speciousness, vagueness, and confusion of motive, he will sadly acknowledge that his net result is simply nothing. A Remnant were here, building a substratum like coral insects; so much he knows, but he will find nothing to put him on the track of who and where and how many they were and what their work was like.

Concerning all this, too, the prophet of the present knows precisely as much and as little as the historian of the future; and that, I repeat, is what makes his job seem to me so profoundly interesting. One of the most suggestive episodes recounted in the Bible is that of a prophet's attempt—the only attempt of the kind on record, I believe—to count up the Remnant. Elijah had fled from persecution into the desert, where the Lord presently overhauled him and asked what he was doing so far away from his job.

He said that he was running away, not because he was a coward, but because all the Remnant had been killed off except himself. He had got away only by the skin of his teeth, and, he being now all the Remnant there was, if he were killed the True Faith would go flat. The Lord replied that he need not worry about that, for even without him the True Faith could probably manage to squeeze along somehow if it had to; "and as for your figures on the Remnant," He said, "I don't mind telling you that there are seven thousand of them back there in Israel whom it seems you have not heard of, but you may take My word for it that there they are."

At that time, probably the population of Israel could not have run to much more than a million or so; and a Remnant of seven thousand out of a million is a highly encouraging percentage for any prophet. With seven thousand of the boys on his side, there was no great reason for Elijah to feel lonesome; and incidentally, that would be something for the modern prophet of the Remnant to think of when he has a touch of the blues. But the main point is that if Elijah the Prophet could not make a closer guess on the number of the Remnant than he made when he missed it by seven thousand, anyone else who tackled the problem would only waste his time.

The other certainty which the prophet of the Remnant may always have is that the Remnant will find him. He may rely on that with absolute assurance. They will find him without his doing anything about it; in fact, if he tries to do anything about it, he is pretty sure to put them off. He does not need to advertise for them nor resort to any schemes of publicity to get their attention. If he is a preacher or a public speaker, for example, he may be quite indifferent to going on show at receptions, getting his picture printed in the newspapers, or furnishing autobiographical material for publication on the side of "human interest." If a writer, he need not make a point of attending any pink teas, autographing books at wholesale, nor entering into any specious freemasonry with reviewers.

All this and much more of the same order lies in the regular and necessary routine laid down for the prophet of the masses. It is, and must be, part of the great general technique of getting the mass-man's ear—or as our vigorous and excellent publicist, Mr. H. L. Mencken, puts it, the technique of boob-bumping. The prophet of the Remnant is not bound to this technique. He may be quite sure that the Remnant will make their own way to him without any adventitious aids; and not only so, but if they find him employing such aids, as I said, it is ten to one that they will smell a rat in them and will sheer off.

The certainty that the Remnant will find him, however, leaves the prophet as much in the dark as ever, as helpless as ever in the matter of putting any estimate of any kind upon the Remnant; for, as appears in the case of Elijah, he remains ignorant of who they are that have found him or where they are or how many. They do not write in and tell him about it, after the manner of those who admire the vedettes of Hollywood, nor yet do they seek him out and attach themselves to his person. They are not that kind. They take his message much as drivers take the directions on a roadside signboard—that is, with very little thought about the sign-board, beyond being gratefully glad that it happened to be there, but with very serious thought about the directions.

This impersonal attitude of the Remnant wonderfully enhances the interest of the imaginative prophet's job. Once in a while, just about often enough to keep his intellectual curiosity in good working order, he will quite accidentally come upon some distinct reflection of his own message in an unsuspected quarter. This enables him to entertain himself in his leisure moments with agreeable speculations about the course his message may have taken in reaching that particular quarter, and about what came of it after it got there. Most interesting of all are those instances, if one could only run them down (but one may always speculate about them), where the recipient himself no longer knows where nor when nor from whom he got the message—or even where, as sometimes happens, he has forgotten that he got it anywhere and imagines that it is all a self-sprung idea of his own.

Such instances as these are probably not infrequent, for, without presuming to enroll ourselves among the Remnant, we can all no doubt remember having found ourselves suddenly under the influence of an idea, the source of which we cannot possibly identify. "It came to us afterward," as we say; that is, we are aware of it only after it has shot up full-grown in our minds, leaving us quite ignorant of how and when and by what agency it was planted there and left to germinate. It seems highly probable that the prophet's message often takes some such course with the Remnant.

If, for example, you are a writer or a speaker or a preacher, you put forth an idea which lodges in the *Unbewusstsein* of a casual member of the Remnant and sticks fast there. For some time it is inert; then it begins to fret and fester until presently it invades the man's conscious mind and, as one might say, corrupts it. Meanwhile, he has quite forgotten how he came by the idea in the first instance, and even perhaps thinks he has invented it; and in those circumstances, the most interesting thing of all is that you never know what the pressure of that idea will make him do.

Part Six

In Retrospect and Prospect

T he foregoing chapters have spelled out in some detail the economic, political and moral aspects of the freedom philosophy, with suggestions as to how the ideal may be put to personal practice.

Comes now time to let Leonard Read recount the miracle of freedom as formed in the life story of a lowly lead pencil.

14

I, Pencil

by Leonard E. Read

To summarize the philosophy of freedom and marvel at the results, one must wonder at the mystery of the creation of so simple an item as a lead pencil.

Here is a pencil's story as told to Leonard Read in 1958. The pencil's official name is "Mongol 482." Its many ingredients are assembled, fabricated, and finished in Eberhard Faber Pencil Company, Wilkes-Barre, Pennsylvania.

I am a lead pencil—the ordinary wooden pencil familiar to all boys and girls and adults who can read and write. Writing is both my vocation and my avocation; that's all I do.

You may wonder why I should write a genealogy. Well, to begin with, my story is interesting. And, next, I am a mystery—more so than a tree or a sunset or even a flash of lightning. But, sadly, I am taken for granted by those who use me, as if I were a mere incident and without background. This supercilious attitude relegates me to the level of the commonplace. This is a species of the grievous error in which mankind cannot too long persist without peril. For, the wise G. K. Chesterton observed, "We are perishing for want of wonder, not for want of wonders."

I, Pencil, simple though I appear to be, merit your wonder and awe, a claim I shall attempt to prove. In fact, if you can understand me—no, that's too much to ask of anyone—if you can become aware of the miraculousness which I symbolize, you can help save the freedom mankind is so unhappily losing. I have a profound lesson to teach. And I can teach this lesson better than can an automobile or an airplane or a mechanical dishwasher because—well, because I am seemingly so simple.

Simple? Yet, *not a single person on the face of this earth knows how to make me.* This sounds fantastic, doesn't it? Especially when it is realized that there are about one and one-half billion of my kind produced in the U.S.A. each year.

Pick me up and look me over. What do you see? Not much meets the eye—there's some wood, lacquer, the printed labeling, graphite lead, a bit of metal, and an eraser.

Innumerable Antecedents

Just as you cannot trace your family tree back very far, so is it impossible for me to name and explain all my antecedents. But I would like to suggest enough of them to impress upon you the richness and complexity of my background.

My family tree begins with what in fact is a tree, a cedar of straight grain that grows in Northern California and Oregon. Now contemplate all the saws and trucks and rope and the countless other gear used in harvesting and carting the cedar logs to the railroad siding. Think of all the persons and the numberless skills that went into their fabrication: the mining of ore, the making of steel and its refinement into saws, axes, motors; the growing of hemp and bringing it through all the stages to heavy and strong rope; the logging camps with their beds and mess halls, the cookery and the raising of all the foods. Why, untold thousands of persons had a hand in every cup of coffee the loggers drink!

The logs are shipped to a mill in San Leandro, California. Can you imagine the individuals who make flat cars and rails and railroad engines and who construct and install the communication systems incidental thereto? These legions are among my antecedents.

Consider the millwork in San Leandro. The cedar logs are cut into small, pencil-length slats less than one-fourth of an inch in thickness. These are kiln dried and then tinted for the same reason women put rouge on their faces. People prefer that I look pretty, not a pallid white. The slats are waxed and kiln dried again. How many skills went into the making of the tint and the kilns, into supplying the heat, the light and power, the belts, motors, and all the other things a mill requires? Sweepers in the mill among my ancestors? Yes, and included are the men who poured the concrete for the dam of a Pacific Gas & Electric Company hydroplant which supplies the mill's power!

Don't overlook the ancestors present and distant who have a hand in transporting sixty carloads of slats across the nation from California to Wilkes-Barre!

Complicated Machinery

Once in the pencil factory—$4,000,000 in machinery and building, all capital accumulated by thrifty and saving parents of mine—each slat is given eight grooves by a complex machine, after which another machine lays leads in every other slat, applies glue, and places another slat atop—a lead sandwich, so to speak. Seven brothers and I are mechanically carved from this "wood-clinched" sandwich.

My "lead" itself—it contains no lead at all—is complex. The graphite is mined in Sri Lanka. Consider these miners and those who make their many tools and the makers of the paper sacks in which the graphite is shipped and those who make the string that ties the sacks and those who put them aboard ships and those who make the ships. Even the lighthouse keepers along the way assisted in my birth—and the harbor pilots.

The graphite is mixed with clay from Mississippi in which ammonium hydroxide is used in the refining process. Then wetting agents are added such as sulfonated tallow—animal fats chemically reacted with sulfuric acid. After passing through numerous machines, the mixture finally appears as endless extrusions—as from a sausage grinder—cut to size, dried, and baked for several hours at 1,850 degrees Fahrenheit. To increase their strength and smoothness the leads are then treated with a hot mixture which includes candelilla wax from Mexico, paraffin wax, and hydrogenated natural fats.

My cedar receives six coats of lacquer. Do you know all of the ingredients of lacquer? Who would think that the growers of castor beans and the refiners of castor oil are a part of it? They are. Why, even the processes by which the lacquer is made a beautiful yellow involve the skills of more persons than one can enumerate!

Observe the labeling. That's a film formed by applying heat to carbon black mixed with resins. How do you make resins and what, pray, is carbon black?

My bit of metal—the ferrule—is brass. Think of all the persons who mine zinc and copper and those who have the skills to make shiny sheet brass from these products of nature. Those black rings on my ferrule are black nickel. What is black nickel and how is it applied? The complete story of why the center of my ferrule has no black nickel on it would take pages to explain.

Then there's my crowning glory, inelegantly referred to in the trade as "the plug," the part man uses to erase the errors he makes with me. An ingredient called "factice" is what does the erasing. It is a rubber-like product made by reacting rape seed oil from the Dutch East Indies with sulfur chloride. Rubber, contrary to the common notion, is only for binding purposes. Then, too, there are numerous vulcanizing and accelerating agents. The pumice comes from Italy; and the pigment which gives "the plug" its color is cadmium sulfide.

No One Knows

Does anyone wish to challenge my earlier assertion that no single person on the face of this earth knows how to make me?

Actually, millions of human beings have had a hand in my creation, no one of whom even knows more than a very few of the others. Now, you may say that I go too far in relating the picker of a coffee berry in far off Brazil and food growers elsewhere to my creation, that this is an extreme position. I shall stand by my claim. There isn't a single person in all these millions, including the president of the pencil company, who contributes more than a tiny, infinitesimal bit of know-how. From the standpoint of know-how the only difference between the miner of graphite in Sri Lanka and the logger in Oregon is in the *type* of know-how. Neither the miner nor the logger can be dispensed with, any more than can the chemist at the factory or the worker in the oil field— paraffin being a by-product of petroleum.

Here is an astounding fact: Neither the worker in the oil field nor the chemist nor the digger of graphite or clay nor any who mans or makes the ships or trains or trucks nor the one who runs the machine that does the knurling on my bit of metal nor the president of the company performs his singular task because he wants me. Each one wants me less, perhaps, than does a child in the first grade. Indeed, there are some among this vast multitude who never saw a pencil nor would they know how to use one. Their motivation is other than me. Perhaps it is something like this: Each of these millions sees that he can thus exchange his tiny know-how for the goods and services he needs or wants. I may or may not be among these items.

No Master Mind

There is a fact still more astounding: the absence of a master mind, of anyone dictating or forcibly directing these countless actions which bring me into being. No trace of such a person can be found. Instead, we find the Invisible Hand at work. This is the mystery to which I earlier referred.

It has been said that "only God can make a tree." Why do we agree with this? Isn't it because we realize that we ourselves could not make one? Indeed, can we even describe a tree? We cannot, except in superficial terms. We can say, for instance, that a certain molecular configuration manifests itself as a tree. But what mind is there among men that could even record, let alone direct, the constant changes in molecules that transpire in the life span of a tree? Such a feat is utterly unthinkable!

I, Pencil, am a complex combination of miracles: a tree, zinc, copper, graphite, and so on. But to these miracles which manifest themselves in Nature an even more extraordinary miracle has been added: the configuration of creative human energies—millions of tiny know-hows configurating naturally and spontaneously in response to human necessity and desire and *in the absence of any human master-minding!* Since only God can make a tree, I insist that only God could make me. Man can no more direct these millions of know-hows to bring me into being than he can put molecules together to create a tree.

The above is what I meant when writing, "If you can become aware of the miraculousness which I symbolize, you can help save the freedom mankind is so unhappily losing." For, if one is aware that these know-hows will naturally, yes, automatically, arrange themselves into creative and productive patterns in response to human necessity and demand—that is, in the absence of governmental or any other coercive master-minding—then one will possess an absolutely essential ingredient for freedom: *a faith in free men*. Freedom is impossible without this faith.

Once government has had a monopoly of a creative activity such, for instance, as the delivery of the mails, most individuals will believe that the mails could not be efficiently delivered by men acting freely. And here is the reason: Each one acknowledges that he himself doesn't know how to do all the things incident to mail delivery. He also recognizes that no other individual could do it. These assumptions are correct. No individual possesses enough know-how to perform a nation's mail delivery any more than any individual possesses enough know-how to make a pencil. Now, in the absence of faith in free men—in the unawareness that millions of tiny know-hows would naturally and miraculously form and cooperate to satisfy this necessity—the individual cannot help but reach the erroneous conclusion that mail can be delivered only by governmental "master-minding."

Testimony Galore

If I, Pencil, were the only item that could offer testimony on what men can accomplish when free to try, then those with little faith would have a fair case. However, there is testimony galore; it's all about us and on every hand. Mail delivery is exceedingly simple when compared, for instance, to the making of an automobile or a calculator or a grain combine or a milling machine or to tens of thousands of other things.

The lesson I have to teach is this: *Leave all creative energies uninhibited*. Merely organize society to act in harmony with this lesson. Let society's legal apparatus remove all obstacles the best it can. Permit these creative know-hows freely to flow. Have faith that free men will respond to the Invisible Hand. This faith will be confirmed. I, Pencil, seemingly simple though I am, offer the miracle of my creation as testimony that this is a practical faith, as practical as the sun, the rain, a cedar tree, the good earth.

Summing Up

Knowledge is widely dispersed throughout the world. No one can possibly grasp all the discrete bits of information that exist in the minds of countless individuals. No one can know whence will come a new idea—for better ways of doing things, for new explanations of reality, for new understanding of the mysteries of the world in which we live. Yet access to such widely scattered information is necessary if the world's resources are to be used effectively to satisfy the needs and wants of individuals.

Only as men are free, do they have the opportunity to choose, to try various ways of doing things, to explore, to experiment, to learn. Only as men are free to exchange goods, services, and ideas with others, can they tap into the knowledge others possess through the market, and benefit from the widely scattered information which exists in the minds of countless individuals. Only as men are free, do they have the opportunity and the incentive to compete in the effort to better their own and their family's situation.

We owe our expanded knowledge of the universe and our increased understanding of nature to the relative freedom our ancestors enjoyed throughout millennia, freedom to question and to investigate things they couldn't explain. We owe our many modern conveniences to the relative freedom our ancestors enjoyed, freedom to experiment, explore, struggle, and compete, freedom to work, save, invest, and use their own private property to develop their ideas and pursue their dreams. It is the relative freedom we still have today that permits today's enterprising individuals to continue to expand our knowledge of the universe and to provide us with advantages our ancestors never knew.

Insofar as individuals are free, they can learn a great deal from experience. From trial and error, they can learn much about moral behavior, individual responsibility, kindness, and respect for the rights and property of others. Even the concept of morality itself depends on freedom. As F. A. Harper writes in this anthology:

> One cannot be truly moral except as there exists the option of being immoral, and except as he selects the moral rather than the immoral option. In the admirable words of Thomas Davidson: "That which is not free is not responsible, and that which is not responsible is not moral."

Through trial and error, individuals can learn how best to gain the cooperation of others. Striving under freedom helps to foster personal responsibility, initiative, innovativeness, social cooperation, voluntary transactions, peaceful interpersonal relations. Thus, freedom is compatible with human nature; it fosters peaceful cooperation; and it promotes economic efficiency and production.

About the Foundation for Economic Education

The Foundation for Economic Education, founded in 1946 by Leonard E. Read, exists to serve individuals concerned about freedom. Recognizing that the real reasons for freedom are grasped only through an understanding of the free market, private property, limited government way of life, the Foundation is a first-source institution providing literature and activities presenting this point of view.

- *The Freeman*, a monthly study journal of ideas on liberty, has been published by the Foundation since 1956. Its articles and essays offer timeless ideas on the positive case for human liberty and criticisms of the failures of collectivism. *The Freeman* is available to anyone upon request. (The extra costs of mailing to any foreign address require a minimum charge of $10.00 per year.)
- Our annual catalogue, *A Literature of Freedom*, carries a wide range of books and audio and video cassette tapes on a variety of topics related to the freedom philosophy. More than 120 volumes are currently available from the Foundation.
- FEE's seminar program brings individuals together to explore free market ideas. In addition to three week-long seminars at FEE each summer, several one- and two-day sessions are offered at FEE and at different locations in the United States. The seminar faculty, composed of FEE staff members and guest lecturers, cover economic, philosophical, and historical topics. Discussion sessions provide valuable opportunities to question and explore ideas.
- High school and college students. We actively encourage the study of free market ideas in high schools and colleges in a number of different ways:

   On-campus lectures by FEE staff members. Groups vary in size from small classes to school-wide assemblies. Lectures are always followed by a question and answer session.

   Seminars in Irvington. Each year FEE hosts two-day seminars for selected undergraduates from around the nation. These seminars present a solid introduction to free market economics and the philosophy of limited government and individual responsibility.

   Debate materials. FEE assists high school debaters by preparing a collection of free market materials covering the current national debate topic. More than 1,000 of these booklets are distributed annually.

For a student subscription to *The Freeman,* or to inquire about any of our other student programs, please write to FEE.

The costs of *The Freeman* and other FEE projects are met through tax-deductible donations. The financial support of more than 10,500 individuals permits the Foundation to distribute its publications widely and to advance the prospects for freedom in America. Join us in this important work!

For further information, write:
The Foundation for Economic Education, Inc.
Irvington-on-Hudson, New York 10533
(914) 591-7230